You Can Be a Stock Market Genius

(Even if You're Not Too Smart)

Uncover the Secret Hiding Places of Stock Market Profits

Joel Greenblatt

SIMON & SCHUSTER

Simon & Schuster
Rockefeller Center
1230 Avenue of the Americas
New York, NY 10020

Simon & Schuster and colophon are registered trademarks
of Simon & Schuster Inc.

Designed by Jeanette Olender
Manufactured in the United States of America

3   5   7   9   10   8   6   4

Library of Congress Cataloging-in-Publication Data
Greenblatt, Joel.
You can be a stock market genius (even if you're not
too smart): uncover the secret hiding places of
stock market profits / Joel Greenblatt
p. cm.
Includes index.
1. Stocks—United States—Handbooks, manuals, etc.
2. Investments—United States—Handbooks, manuals, etc.   I. Title.
HG4921.G718   1997
332.63'22—dc21   96-50310   CIP
ISBN 0-684-83213-5

ACKNOWLEDGMENTS

As with any work of this kind, many people deserve the blame. Of course, the ultimate responsibility for errors, omissions, misstatements, or misguided advice rests with some guy from Cleveland who no one can seem to find. As a consequence, I have no choice but to point the finger at the following suspects:

The entire cast and crew at Gotham Capital. This includes my partner in crime, Daniel Nir, who I had the good fortune of plucking from the jaws of Harvard Business School at the inception of Gotham Capital—he is one of the primary reasons for Gotham's success, a major contributor and supporter of this project, and still one of my all time best picks; my partner, Robert Goldstein, whose brutally honest (and, unfortunately, fair and insightful) comments made this book far better than it would have been—also special thanks for his unparalleled contributions to many of the examples found on these pages (and to the profits that went with them), including the discovery of Charter Medical and his exceptional work on Host Marriott and Liberty Media;

my partner, Edward (Ned) Grier, for both his helpful comments and superior research efforts on many of the case studies found herein, including General Dynamics and Strattec. While each of these extraordinary investors could have compiled a spectacular investment record without the aid of any partners, I feel privileged to have had the opportunity to work with such a talented group of friends.

Speaking of talent and friends, I would also like to give special thanks to Gotham's dedicated and fearless head (and only) trader, Lisa Alpert; our chief financial officer and all around nice guy, Bruce Berkowitz (no relation to the Wells Fargo investor by the same name); and our special and multi-talented office manager, Alison Jarret.

Two more people deserve special mention as members of the Gotham family. The first, Bruce Newberg, has truly been a full partner in Gotham's success. He is not only responsible for raising the start-up capital that made Gotham possible, but for contributing a never-ending stream of sage advice, exceptional investment ideas, and overwhelming friendship as well. Everyone should be lucky enough to have such a loyal and good friend. The second Gotham family member also happens to double as my sister. Linda Greenblatt has been the primary sounding board and constructive contributor to this book. It's amazing that even after fifteen readings, she still managed to laugh in all the right places *and* found the time to make her new investment partnership, Saddle Rock Partners, a major success. Her infinite patience, dedication, and intelligence has had a dramatic effect on the final result. I absolutely couldn't have finished this project without Linda's help.

Other likely suspects, owing to their significant contributions and friendship, include: John Scully of Hamilton Partners and Columbia Business School, a mentor and friend from my Halcyon days; Eric Rosenfeld, Managing Director of Oppenheimer & Co.; Jeffrey Schwarz, Managing Partner of Metropolitan Capital Advisors; Richard Pzena, Pzena Investment Management; Mitch Julis, Managing Partner of Canyon Partners; Seth Klarman, President of the Baupost Group; Joseph Mazzella, my attorney and a partner at Lane, Altman & Owens; Robert Kushel, my broker at Smith Barney; Mark Gimpel, Esq., for my glorious Apache Relay memories; Major Gary E. Warren, U.S.M.C. for his counting humor; and Rabbi Label Lam, for his invaluable directions towards the stake in the sand, and specifically, for his "currency of life" thoughts in the final chapter.

Special thanks also to Bob Rosenkranz, chairman of Delphi Financial Group and managing partner of Acorn Partners, for his unrivaled support of Gotham throughout the years; Ezra Merkin, our partner at Gotham for two and a half years during the 1980s; and Stan Kaplan, Gotham's head trader for our first five years.

Thank you also to Bob Mecoy, my editor at Simon & Schuster; Sandra Dijkstra, my agent; and Guy Kettelhack, for his assistance with the original book proposal.

Extra special thanks for the love, support and encouragement of my entire family, each of whom pitched in to add significantly to the final result (me *and* the book): my wonderful parents, Allan and Muriel Greenblatt; Richard and Amy Greenblatt; Drs. Gary and Sharon Curhan; and my in-laws (*the* in-laws) Dr. George and Cecile Teebor.

Grateful appreciation also to my son, whose searing question, "So, what are you, Dad? Policeman? Fireman? What?" served as a major inspiration for the completion of this book. At least, now I can respond, "You know what Dr. Seuss does, right?"

Finally, to Julie, the love of my life (and my wife), and our three unbelievable children, thank you for the gift of each precious day together.

To my wonderful wife, Julie,

and our three magnificent spinoffs

Contents

You Can Be a
Stock Market
Genius

Chapter 1

FOLLOW THE YELLOW
BRICK ROAD—

THEN HANG A RIGHT

It doesn't make sense that a book can teach you how to make a fortune in the stock market. After all, what chance do you have for success when you're up against an army of billion-dollar portfolio managers or a horde of freshly trained MBAs? A contest between you, the proud owner of a $24 "how to" book, and these guys hardly seems fair.

The truth is, it isn't fair. The well-heeled Wall Street money managers and the hotshot MBA's don't have a chance against you and this book. No, you won't find any magic formula in chapter 8, and this isn't a sequel to *How to Succeed in Business Without Really Trying*, but if you're willing to invest a reasonable amount of time and effort, stock market profits, and even a fortune, await.

Okay: What's the catch? If it's so easy, why can't the MBAs and the pros beat your pants off? Clearly, they put in their share of time and effort, and while they may not all be rocket scientists, there aren't many village idiots among them either.

As strange as it may seem, there is no catch. The answer

to this apparent paradox—why you potentially have the power to beat the pants off the so-called market "experts"—lies in a study of academic thinking, the inner workings of Wall Street, and the weekend habits of my in-laws.

We start with some good news about your education: simply put, if your goal is to beat the market, an MBA or a Ph.D. from a top business school will be of virtually no help. Well, it's good news, that is, if you haven't yet squandered tons of time and money at a business school in the single-minded quest for stock market success. In fact, the basic premise of most academic theory is this: It is not possible to beat the market consistently other than by luck.

This theory, usually referred to as the efficient-market or "random-walk" theory, suggests that thousands of investors and analysts take in all the publicly available information on a particular company, and through their decisions to buy and sell that company's stock establish the "correct" trading price. In effect, since stocks are more or less efficiently priced (and therefore, you can't consistently find bargain-priced stocks), it is not possible to outperform the market averages over long periods of time. Although exceptions (e.g., the January effect, small size effects and low price/earnings strategies) are covered briefly by the academics, most of these "market-beating" strategies are dismissed as trivial, transient, or difficult to achieve after factoring in taxes and transaction costs.

Since beating the market is out of the question, finance

professors spend a lot of time teaching things like quadratic parametric programming—which, loosely translates to how to pick diversified stock portfolios in three-dimensional space. In other words, if you muddle through complex mathematical formulas and throw in a little calculus and statistical theory along the way, you stand a pretty good chance of matching the performance of the popular market averages. Wow! While there are plenty of other bells and whistles, the message is clear: You can't beat the market, so don't even try. Thousands of MBA's and Ph.D.'s have paid good money for this lousy advice.

There are two reasons not to accept the basic teachings of the professors. First, there are some fundamental flaws in the assumptions and methodology used by the academics—flaws we'll look at briefly later on, but which are not the central focus of this book. Second, and more important, even if the professors are generally correct and the market for stocks is more or less efficient, their studies and conclusions do not apply to *you*.

Obviously, most of Wall Street must also ignore the academics because the whole concept of getting paid for your investment advice, whether through commissions or investment advisory fees, doesn't square too well with the idea that the advice really isn't worth anything. Unfortunately for the professionals, the facts would seem to support the conclusions of the academics. If academic theory held true, you would expect the long-term record of pension and mutual-fund managers to equal the performance of the market averages reduced by the amount of the advisory fee. In a slight deviation from efficient-market theory, the professionals actually do approximately 1 percent worse per year than the relevant market averages, even before deducting their management fees. Does the theory that markets are "more or less" efficient explain this disappointing performance on the part of professionals, or are there other factors at work that lead to these lackluster results?

THE PROFESSIONAL'S CHALLENGE

I spoke with a professional whom I consider one of the best in the business, a friend I'll call Bob (even though his real name is Rich). Bob is in charge of $12 billion of U.S. equity funds at a major investment firm. For some perspective, if you went to the racetrack and placed a bet with $100 bills, $12 billion would stack twenty World Trade Centers high (needless to say, a bet that would almost certainly kill the odds on your horse). According to Bob, the bottom line and the measure of his success is this: How does the return on his portfolio stack up against the return of the Standard & Poor's 500 average? In fact, Bob's record is phenomenal: over the past ten years his average annual return has exceeded the return of the S&P 500 by between 2 and 3 percent.

At first blush, the word "phenomenal" and an increased annual yield of 2 or 3 percent seem somewhat incongruous. Though it is true that after twenty years of compounding even 2 percent extra per year creates a 50 percent larger nest egg, this is not why Bob's returns are phenomenal. Bob's performance is impressive because in the world of billion-dollar portfolios, this level of excess return is incredibly hard to come by on a consistent basis. Some quick calculations help expose the limitations imposed on Bob by the sheer size of his portfolio. Imagine the dollar investment in each stock position when Bob sets out to divvy up $12 billion. To create a 50-stock portfolio, the average investment in each individual stock would have to be approximately $240 million; for 100 stocks, $120 million.

There are approximately 8,500 stocks listed on the New York Stock Exchange, the American Stock Exchange, and the NASDAQ over-the-counter market combined. Of this number, about 600 stocks have a market capitalization over $2.5 billion and approximately 1200 have market values over $1 billion. If we assume Bob does not care to own more than 10 percent of any company's outstanding shares (for legal and liquidity reasons), it's likely that the minimum number of different stocks Bob will end up with in his portfolio will fall somewhere between 50 and 100. If he chooses to expand the universe from which he chooses potential purchase candidates to those companies with market capitalizations below $1 billion, perhaps to take advantage of some lesser followed and possibly undiscovered bargain stocks, his minimum number could easily expand to over 200 different stocks.

Intuitively, you would probably agree that there is an advantage to holding a diversified portfolio so that one or two unfortunate (read "bonehead") stock picks do not unduly impair your confidence and pocketbook. On the other hand, is the correct number of different stocks to own in a "properly" diversified portfolio 50, 100, or even 200?

It turns out that diversification addresses only a portion (and not the major portion) of the overall risk of investing in the stock market. Even if you took the precaution of owning 8,500 stocks, you would still be at risk for the up and down movement of the entire market. This risk, known as market risk, would not have been eliminated by your "perfect" diversification.

While simply buying more stocks can't help you avoid market risk, it *can* help you avoid another kind of risk—"nonmarket risk." Nonmarket risk is the portion of a stock's risk that is not related to the stock market's overall movements. This type of risk can arise when a company's factory burns down or when a new product doesn't sell as well as expected. By not placing all your eggs in a buggy-whip, breast-implant, pet-rock, or huckapoo-sweater company, you *can* diversify away that portion of your risk that comes from the misfortunes of any individual company.

Statistics say that owning just two stocks eliminates 46 percent of the nonmarket risk of owning just one stock. This type of risk is supposedly reduced by 72 percent with a four-stock portfolio, by 81 percent with eight stocks, 93 percent with 16 stocks, 96 percent with 32 stocks, and 99 percent with 500 stocks. Without quibbling over the accuracy of these particular statistics, two things should be remembered:

1. After purchasing six or eight stocks in different industries, the benefit of adding even more stocks to your portfolio in an effort to decrease risk is small, and

2. Overall market risk will not be eliminated merely by adding more stocks to your portfolio.

From a practical standpoint, when Bob chooses his favorite stocks and is on pick number twenty, thirty, or eighty, he is pursuing a strategy imposed on him by the dollar size of his portfolio, legal issues, and fiduciary considerations, *not* because he feels his last picks are as good as his first or because he needs to own all those stocks for optimum portfolio diversification.

In short, poor Bob has to come up with scores of great stock ideas, choose from a limited universe of the most widely followed stocks, buy and sell large amounts of individual stocks without affecting their share prices, and perform in a fish bowl where his returns are judged quarterly and even monthly.

Luckily, you don't.

THE SECRET TO YOUR FORTUNE

Since Bob clearly has his hands full, where can an investor turn for insight into making a fortune in the stock market? For better or worse, all roads appear to leave us at the doorstep of my in-laws. (Don't worry, I said mine—not yours.)

A typical weekend will find them scouting out a country auction, antique store, or estate sale looking for art or antiques that catch their fancy. As avid collectors, they seek out works that will give them joy to own and live with on a daily basis. As closet capitalists, they look for undiscovered or unrecognized works of art or antiques that they can buy at prices far below true value.

When in capitalist mode, the in-laws follow a very simple strategy. Whether they find a beautiful specimen of antique furniture at Podunk Fine Antiques & Tractor Parts or an impressionist painting from Grandma Bagodonuts' attic, they ask themselves only one question before buying. Are there comparable pieces of furniture or paintings that have recently sold at auction (or to dealers) at prices far above the potential purchase price?

It's truly that simple, although we can probably learn more from the questions they don't ask. They don't ask, "Is this painter going to be the next Picasso?" or "Is eighteenth-century French furniture going to skyrocket in value?" While it would be nice and perhaps more lucrative to be able to predict those types of future developments, few people can combine the ability, knowledge, and timing to foresee and profit consistently from future events. Whether the in-laws can or cannot predict the future is beside the point; they don't have to—they already know how to profit from studying the present.

That doesn't mean their knowledge of art and antiques doesn't help them to make money, but many people can acquire that same knowledge. Their edge comes from taking this knowledge and applying it in places off the beaten path. While these places are tougher to find, once found, less competition from other informed collectors creates an opportunity for them to find "inefficiently" priced bargains.

Finding bargain stocks works much the same way. If you spend your energies looking for and analyzing situations not closely followed by other informed investors, your chance of finding bargains greatly increases. The trick is locating those opportunities.

It's like the old story about the plumber who comes to your house, bangs on the pipes once, and says, "That'll be a hundred dollars."

"A hundred dollars!" you say. "All you did was bang on the pipes once!"

"Oh no," the plumber responds. "Banging on the pipes is only five dollars. Knowing where to bang—that's ninety-five dollars."

In the stock market, knowing where to "bang" is the secret to your fortune. With that in mind, let's uncover some of the secret hiding places of stock-market profits.

Chapter 2

SOME BASICS—

DON'T LEAVE HOME
WITHOUT THEM

When I was fifteen, the only gambling establishment that would let me sneak in was the Hollywood Dog Track. This was a great thing because, during my first illicit visit, I discovered a sure-fire route to big greyhound riches. In the third race, there was a dog who had run each of his previous six races in only thirty-two seconds. The odds on this dog—we'll call him "Lucky"—were 99–1. None of the dogs up against Lucky in the third race had managed a time better than forty-four seconds in any previous race.

Of course, I bet what passed for a small fortune at the time on Lucky to WIN. If all those fools who bet on the other dogs wanted to give me their money, so be it. However, as Lucky straggled down the home stretch in last place, my opinion of the other gamblers slowly began to change.

This was Lucky's first race at a longer distance. Apparently, as everyone else already knew, Lucky's spectacularly fast times in his previous races were achieved at much shorter distances. All the other dogs were experienced long-distance runners. My 99–1 sure thing was a mirage that quickly evaporated along with my money.

On the bright side, in less than a minute I learned a valuable lesson. Without a basic level of knowledge and understanding, you can't tell a great investment from a real dog. So before you start hunting in the stock market's back alleys for hidden investment jewels, here are some basics that should help in the search.

A FEW BASICS

1. DO YOUR OWN WORK

There are really two reasons to do your own work. The first is pretty simple. You have no choice. If you are truly looking at situations that others are ignoring, there will rarely be much media or Wall Street coverage. While there is usually plenty of industry or company information available, some of it quite helpful, almost none will focus on the special attributes that make your investment opportunity attractive. This should be fine with you; "the more the merrier" is not your credo.

The other reason to do your own work is closely related. As much as possible, you don't want to be well paid merely for taking big risks. Anyone can manage that. You want to be well paid because you did your homework. If you are one of the few people to analyze a particular investment opportunity, it follows that you are in the best position to assess the appropriate payoff for the risk taken. Not all obscure or hidden investment opportunities are attractive. The idea is to place your "bets" in situations where the rewards promise to greatly outweigh the risks.

Naturally, everyone would like to invest in situations where the odds are stacked in their favor. But most people can't because they don't know these special opportunities exist. The payoff to all your legwork and analysis is the opportunity to invest in situations that offer unfair economic returns. Your extraordinary profits will not be a result of taking on big risks; they will be the justly deserved pay for doing your homework.

But is it any fun to invest when the odds are unfairly stacked in your favor? You bet it is.

2. DON'T TRUST ANYONE OVER THIRTY

3. DON'T TRUST ANYONE THIRTY OR UNDER

Get it? The odds of anyone calling you on the phone with good investment advice are about the same as winning Lotto without buying a ticket. It could happen, but it's not bloody likely. When stockbrokers call or write, take Nancy Reagan's advice: "Just say No." The record of research analysts at major brokerage firms for predicting future earnings or stock prices is quite poor—and if you believe the record of smaller brokerage firms who tout penny stocks is any better, please write me for a refund; you can't be helped. Even institutional clients of reputable investment firms don't get particularly good advice.

The reasons for this consistently poor showing are largely systematic in nature. The vast majority of analysts are not directly paid by clients. The research recommendations and reports produced by these analysts are peddled by the firm's stockbrokers in exchange for commission business. One perennial problem is the overwhelming incentive for analysts to issue "Buy" recommendations. The universe of stocks not owned by a customer is always much larger than the list of those currently owned. Consequently, it's much easier to generate commissions from new "Buy" recommendations than from recommendations to sell.

Another occupational hazard for research analysts is that analysts who pan a company's stock are usually cut off from an important source of information. Crucial contact with company officers and information from investor-relations personnel may well be reserved for other, more "cooperative" analysts. This obviously makes the job more difficult. In addition, the chance of the offending analyst's investment firm capturing future investment-banking assignments from that company is probably slim. This is why popular euphemisms like "source of funds," "hold," and "untimely" are used instead of the more direct "Sell" recommendation.

There are several other problems besides this optimistic bias. It is very difficult to go out on a limb with earnings or stock-price predictions if all your fellow analysts think differently. It's much safer to be wrong in a crowd than to risk being the only one to misread a situation that everyone else pegged correctly. As a result, getting fresh, independent thinking from analysts is the exception, not the norm.

Further, most analysts cover only one industry group. You have chemical analysts, bank analysts, and retail analysts who know little about the comparative investment merits of stocks in other industries. So when a chemical analyst says "Buy" a stock in his industry, he has not compared its investment prospects against stocks in any of fifty other industry groups. A neighborhood in downtown Cleveland may look great next to one three blocks over, but not when compared to Beverly Hills.

Since an analyst's job is to compare companies within particular industry groups, extraordinary corporate events often fall outside an analyst's specific area of expertise. This is true even when these special events, like spinoffs or mergers, involve companies he does follow. Many analysts actually suspend ratings or drop coverage of companies that are undergoing major corporate changes—understandable given their job description, but not too helpful if their real goal is to give profitable investment advice.

The next thing analysts run up against is cold hard economics. It doesn't pay for Wall Street analysts to cover stocks or investment situations unless they can generate enough revenue (read commissions or future investment-banking fees) to make the time and effort involved worthwhile. Therefore, smaller capitalization stocks whose shares don't trade in large volumes, obscure securities, and unique situations are generally ignored. Ironically, the very areas that are uneconomic for large firms to explore are precisely the ones that hold the most potential profit for you.

The bottom line is, even if you live in Fantasyland, where fees and commissions have no influence on investment advice, you still must face a harsh reality. Your broker, trustworthy or not, has no idea how to invest your money. But don't blame him, even if he is over thirty. It's the system, man: it just doesn't work.

Still want a hot tip from someone you can trust? Okay— *psst*—bet Lucky in the third at Hollywood.

4. PICK YOUR SPOTS

The highlight of summer camp was Color War. For the uninitiated, Color War was a week-long ritual each summer in which the entire camp was divided into two teams, the Blue and the Gray. The teams then competed, by age group, for the most victories in a variety of sports. The highlight of Color War was something called the Apache Relay. This was a single race at the end of Color War pitting one team encompassing all age groups against the other. Every camper, domino-style, had an individual athletic challenge or bizarre task to complete before the next camper on his team could attempt his own feat.

So, like the Apache warriors of old, one by one, campers would compete in events from simple running and swimming to pie eating (with hands tied behind the back) and walking with an egg balanced on a spoon stuck between the teeth. The advantage of one team over the other, unlike some other competitions, did not necessarily hinge on which team had the stronger or faster athletes, but rather on which team had been lucky enough to get David Versotski. David had the task of serving three net serves in Ping-Pong before the next camper on his team could perform a more mundane task like running down to the waterfront.

In Ping-Pong, a net serve is when the ball is served, hits the net, and still manages to land on the other side of the table. All summer long David was just a regular guy, but he could whip these serves off on demand—one, two, three— like nobody else, saving crucial minutes in an Apache relay that was often decided in a matter of seconds. In those tense moments before the race, the buzz around David's team was always something like, "Don't worry—we have Versotski!" I don't know whatever happened to David, but unquestionably, if net serves in Ping-Pong had been a professional or even Olympic sport, the name David Versotski would today be mentioned in the same company with Babe Ruth or Michael Jordan.

What's the point? The point is that if David could arrange it so that any time he competed it would be a contest of who could hit the most net serves, he would do a lot of winning. Unfortunately, life doesn't usually work that way. You can't always choose your battles or your playing field. When it comes to the stock market, though, you can.

This concept has been variously illustrated by the likes of Warren Buffett as "Swing at only one of twenty pitches," "There are no called strikes on Wall Street," or "Wait for your pitch." The most successful horse players (I guess they lose the least) are the ones who don't bet on every race but wager on only those occasions when they have a clear conviction. It makes sense that if you limit your investments to those situations where you are knowledgeable and confident, and only those situations, your success rate will be very high. There is no sense diluting your best ideas or favorite situations by continuing to work your way down a list of attractive opportunities. If "net serves" was only one of the ten events in a newly created decathlon, David's advantage and expertise would be diluted to such an extent that his chances of winning the entire decathlon would be slim. So, if no one stops you from just hitting net serves, keep doing it until they cart you away.

The strategy of putting all your eggs in one basket and watching that basket is less risky than you might think. If you assume, based on past history, that the average annual return from investing in the stock market is approximately 10 percent, statistics say the chance of any year's return falling between −8 percent and +28 percent are about two out of three. In statistical talk, the standard deviation around the market average of 10 percent in any one year is approximately 18 percent. Obviously, there is still a one-out-of-three chance of falling outside this incredibly wide thirty-six-point range (−8 percent to +28 percent). These statistics hold for portfolios containing 50 or 500 different securities (in other words, the type of portfolios held by most stock mutual funds).

What do statistics say you can expect, though, if your port-folio is limited to only *five* securities? The range of expected returns in any one year really must be immense. Who knows how the crazy movements of one or two stocks can skew re-sults? The answer is that there is an approximately two-out-of-three chance that your return will fall in a range of −11 percent to +31 percent. The expected return of the portfolio still remains 10 percent. If there are eight stocks in your port-folio, the range narrows a little further, to −10 percent to +30 percent. Not a significant difference from owning 500 stocks. The fact that you can drive a truck through any of these wide ranges of expected returns should lend comfort to those who don't hold fifty stocks in their portfolio and strike fear in the hearts of anyone who thinks owning dozens of stocks will as-sure them a predictable annual income.

Over the long term (and this could mean twenty or thirty years long), stocks, despite the annual variability in returns, are probably the most attractive investment vehicle. There-fore, owning a widely diversified portfolio of stocks should enable you more or less to mirror the performance of the popular market averages. In the case of stocks, doing average ain't all that bad.

However, if your goal is to do significantly better than av-erage, then picking your spots, swinging at one of twenty pitches, sticking to net serves, or any other metaphor that brings the point home for you, is the way to go. The fact that this highly selective process may leave you with only a hand-ful of positions that fit your strict criteria shouldn't be a problem. The penalty you pay for having a focused port-folio—a slight increase in potential annual volatility—should be far outweighed by your increased long-term returns.

Still not comfortable with the concept of putting a small group of eggs all in one basket? Don't despair. There are other ways to tackle the issue of risk without diluting the effectiveness of investing only in your few favorite situations.

5. DON'T BUY MORE STOCKS; PUT MONEY IN THE BANK

For about $1,000, an insurance company will agree to pay a healthy thirty-five-year-old male $1,000,000 should he be unfortunate enough to die over the next year. The actuarial tables say this is a good bet for the insurance company. But would you take the insurance company's side of the bet? Probably not. The reason is that regardless of what the statistics may indicate, you can't afford to lose $1,000,000—especially for a crummy thousand bucks. The insurance company, on the other hand, by pooling thousands of policy-holders together can create a portfolio of underwritten risks that do follow the statistical tables. That's why they can make a good business out of consistently booking bets that you, as an individual, can't afford to take.

In effect, a specific risk, when viewed in isolation, may appear unsafe or even foolish, but in the context of an entire portfolio, the same risk can make good sense. So, if that's true and spreading your risks around is such a good idea, why do I keep telling you that owning just a few stocks is the way to go?

The answer comes in two parts. First, on each individual policy, the insurance company was risking a loss of $1,000 for every $1 bet. It would take many thousands of similar policies over a period of years to make this bet worthwhile. Fortunately, the risks you assume by purchasing individual stocks are limited to a $1 loss for each $1 invested. As a result, you can prudently invest in only a handful of attractive stocks without being accused of taking crazy risks. But everyone else advises maintaining a widely diversified portfolio; how can you be expected to "go for it" by focusing on only a few selected stock-market opportunities?

The answer, and the other reason why a widely diversified stock portfolio isn't a magic formula for avoiding risk, can be found in the way you should be thinking about your stock investments from the start. It's important to remember that for many people a stock portfolio is only a portion of their entire investment holdings. Most people have a portion of their net worth in the bank or in money-market funds, in their homes, in bonds, in the value of their life-insurance policies, or in investment real estate, to name a few likely places. If you're looking to avoid putting all your eggs in one basket, this broader type of diversification, over varying asset classes, will accomplish that goal more effectively than merely diversifying your stock portfolio. In other words, don't screw up a perfectly good stock-market strategy by diversifying your way into mediocre returns.

In fact, no matter how many different stocks you buy, investing in the stock market with money that you will need over the next two or three years to help with rent or mortgage payments, food, medical care, tuition, or other necessities is risky in the first place. Remember, the potential swings in stock-market returns from year to year are huge anyway, even if you diversify to the extent of owning all 8,000+ stocks. Rest assured, the practice of selling stocks when you need the money holds little promise as an effective investment method.

Ideally, your decisions to buy and sell stocks should be based solely on the investment merits. This may mean leaving that extra money in the bank or in other assets, even if you've made up your mind that stocks are the investment vehicle of choice. Leaving some of your assets on the sidelines (i.e., out of the stock market) should be your compromise to prudent diversification. As long as you're willing to do your own homework, a strategy of owning a select handful of your favorite stock situations should yield results far superior to a strategy of owning dozens of different stocks or mutual funds.

From time to time, this selective strategy may result in slightly wider swings in performance than a strategy based on owning a few shares of everything, or what's known as an indexing approach. However, if you have arranged your overall portfolio of assets so that you can weather the inevitable market downswings without being forced to sell, this slight difference shouldn't matter. What should matter is that over a period of even five or ten years, you can have your cake and eat it, too. During those years, you will have invested in dozens of different investment situations (although in only a handful at any one time), thereby getting plenty of diversification with superior returns to boot.

6. LOOK DOWN, NOT UP

One cherished and immutable law of investing is that there is a trade-off between risk and reward. The more risk you assume in your portfolio, academics and most professionals agree, the more reward you receive in the form of higher returns. The less risk assumed, the lower the return. In short, you can't get something (high returns) for nothing (taking low risks). This concept is so fundamental that it provides the underpinning for the investment strategies of both academics and professionals.

Of course, if the discussion ended there, you could just dial up your desired level of risk and receive the targeted return you deserve. In a perfectly efficient world, this relationship between risk and reward should hold true. Obviously, since you will be looking for pockets of opportunity where there are inefficiently priced investments (i.e., stocks or investment situations so far off the beaten path that analysts and investors have not priced them correctly), this immutable relationship between risk and reward should not apply.

That, however, does not make the concept of risk/reward irrelevant to you. Far from it. It is perhaps the most important investment concept of all. That's why it's so amazing that, at least when it comes to analyzing the risks of individual stocks, most professionals and academics get it wrong. They get it wrong because they measure the "risk" portion of risk/reward in an erroneous and truly puzzling way.

Risk, according to generally accepted wisdom, is defined as the risk of receiving volatile returns. In the academic world, risk is measured by a stock's "beta"—the price volatility of a particular stock relative to the market as a whole. Usually the calculation of "beta" is based on an extrapolation of a stock's past price volatility. In this topsy-turvy world, the distinction between upside volatility and downside volatility is greatly confused: a stock that moves up significantly over the course of a year is labeled riskier than a stock that moves down slightly during the same period.

Also, using *past* price movements (or volatility) as the basis for determining the riskiness of a particular stock can often lead to faulty conclusions. A stock that has fallen from 30 to 10 is considered riskier than a stock that has fallen from 12 to 10 in the same period. Although both stocks can now be purchased for $10, the stock which has fallen the farthest, and the one that is now priced at the biggest discount to its recent high price, is still considered the "riskier" of the two. It might be. But it could be that most of the stock's downside risk has been eliminated by the huge price drop. The truth is you can't really tell much of anything just from measuring a stock's past price movements.

In fact, not only doesn't a stock's past price volatility serve as a good indicator of future profitability, it doesn't tell you something much more important—how much you can lose. Let's repeat that: *It doesn't tell you how much you can lose.* Isn't risk of loss what most people care about when they think of risk? Comparing the risk of loss in an investment to the potential gain is what investing is all about.

Perhaps, since the measurement of potential gain and loss from a particular stock is so subjective, it is easier, if you are a professional or academic, to use a concept like volatility as a substitute or a replacement for risk than to use some other measure. Whatever the reason for everyone else's general abdication of common sense, your job remains to quantify, by some measure, a stock's upside and downside. This is such an imprecise and difficult task, though, that a proxy of your own may well be in order.

One way to take on this challenge is to think, once again, in terms of the in-laws. As you recall, if they find a painting selling for $5,000 when a comparable painting by the same artist has recently sold at auction for $10,000, they buy it. The perceived cushion of $5,000 between auction value and purchase price is what Benjamin Graham, the acknowledged father of security analysis, referred to as their "margin of safety." If the in-laws' perceptions are correct, their margin is so large that it is extremely unlikely they will lose money on their new purchase. On the other hand, if their perceptions are somewhat off—the quality of their painting is not quite up to the standard of the one recently

41

auctioned, the $10,000 price was a one-time aberration, or the art market collapses between the time of purchase and the time they get to the auction house—their losses should be minimized by this initial built-in cushion, their margin of safety.

So one way to create an attractive risk/reward situation is to limit downside risk severely by investing in situations that have a large margin of safety. The upside, while still difficult to quantify, will usually take care of itself. In other words, look down, not up, when making your initial investment decision. If you don't lose money, most of the remaining alternatives are good ones. While this basic concept is simple enough, it would be very difficult to devise a complicated mathematical formula to illustrate the point. Then again, not much downside to that . . .

7. THERE'S MORE THAN ONE ROAD TO INVESTMENT HEAVEN

There are plenty of ways to achieve substantial wealth through investing in the stock market. Likewise, there are plenty of people who try. There are, however, only a select few who succeed. As Butch and Sundance might say, "Who are those guys and how do they do it?"

One such successful investor, whose methods should be studied closely, has just been mentioned. Benjamin Graham has influenced many investors through his writings and teaching. The concept of "margin of safety" is perhaps his greatest and most enduring contribution to the investing profession. Graham generally used objective measures like a stock's book value (the company's net worth as disclosed on its balance sheet) and its price/earnings ratio (the price of a stock relative to its annual earnings—a.k.a. its P/E ratio) to help calculate a company's true value. His advice was to purchase stocks only when they traded at a significant discount to this value.

When viewing the stock market, Graham said, you should imagine that you are in business with "Mr. Market" and that the price of a stock merely represents the cost of a certain percentage ownership of an entire company. Some days Mr. Market will be inordinately happy and quote you a ridiculously high price for your stock and other days he will be unduly fearful and quote an unreasonably low price. Only at these extremes should you take advantage of Mr. Market and care what he has to say. Otherwise it's best, according to Graham, to forget about the market and concentrate on a company's operating and financial fundamentals.

It seems more than a coincidence that, of the small group of investors who have been extraordinarily successful over long periods of time, most adhere in some form to Graham's concepts of "margin of safety" and "Mr. Market." Even in the area of company valuation, where some have successfully altered or expanded upon Graham's methods, Graham's original concepts have been repeatedly validated. Recent studies (e.g., Lakonishok, Schleifer and Vishny, *Journal of Finance*, December 1994) continue to support his thesis that simply buying stocks that trade at low prices relative to their book values and earnings provides superior long-term results.

According to these studies, a value approach to stock picking, such as Graham's, far surpasses the results achieved by buying the so-called glamour (or most popular) stocks, purchasing stock-market-index funds, or placing money with professional managers. These results can be achieved— contrary to efficient-market theory—without taking on more volatility than other methods, and they apply to both large and small capitalization stocks.

The explanation for this may be that individuals and professionals systematically overrate the long-term prospects of companies that have done well recently, and at the same time underestimate the value of companies that are underperforming or unpopular at the moment. Relying on objective measures like a company's book value and historical earnings to determine value may help eliminate some of the emotional and institutional biases likely to be found in more future-based valuation methods. Even though Graham's methods have been well documented and extensively studied, they continue to yield superior results for those investors who choose to follow them.

Graham's most famous disciple and admirer, Warren Buffett, while a strong proponent of seeking investments with a large margin of safety and of viewing the stock market from the vantage point of Mr. Market, has successfully added his own thoughts about what constitutes value when seeking attractive investments. Primarily, Buffett has found that investing in fundamentally good businesses, as opposed to investing solely in stocks priced cheaply in a strict statistical sense, can add dramatically to investment returns. While this hardly seems an insight worthy of marching bands and fireworks, this seemingly minor modification is the most likely reason why Buffett has become not only Graham's most successful disciple but, by most counts, the world's greatest investor.

Buffett tries to focus on well-managed companies that have a strong franchise, brand name, or market niche. In addition, his investments are concentrated in businesses that he understands well and that possess attractive underlying economic (that is, they generate lots of cash) and competitive characteristics. In this way, when Buffett buys a business at what appears to be an attractive discount to current value, he also benefits from the future increase in value generated by owning all or part of a business that is well situated. Graham's statistical bargains generally do not benefit from this added kicker. In fact, according to Buffett, the risk in buying poor businesses is that much of the bargain element of the initial purchase discount may well be dissipated by the time a catalyst comes along to unlock what appeared to be the initial excess value.

Yet another successful approach to stock-market investing has been championed by perhaps the world's greatest mutual fund manager, Peter Lynch. The Fidelity Magellan Fund, which he ran successfully through 1990, returned $28 for every dollar invested at the start of his tenure in

1977. Through his books, columns, and interviews, Lynch strongly suggests that ordinary individuals can outperform the experts by investing in companies and industries that they already know and understand. Whether you're at the mall, the supermarket, or even the amusement park, new investment prospects are everywhere, according to Lynch. He believes that with a reasonable amount of company research and investigation—the type well within reach of the average investor—everyday insights and experiences can be turned into a profitable stock portfolio.

While not in the same league as a Peter Lynch—he managed $14 billion when he wrote his first book; they managed $90,000—the Beardstown Ladies have run up an enviable record over the approximately ten years since they started an investment club. Their secret weapon: *Value Line*. The *Value Line Investment Survey* is a weekly publication with extensive fundamental and statistical data on approximately 1,700 of the largest public companies. Each week, *Value Line* ranks the stocks in this universe for timeliness and safety. In general, the stocks *Value Line* ranks highest for timeliness (rankings of 1 or 2 on a scale of 5) have handily outperformed the market averages over a thirty-year period. *Value Line* uses a proprietary formula that includes factors like a stock's earnings and price momentum, positive and negative earnings surprises, and certain fundamental attributes to determine its stock rankings. The investment opinions of *Value Line*'s research analysts were once included in the ranking system, but this input was dropped long ago as the system performed better without them.

On the other hand, the Beardstown Ladies, starting from a list of *Value Line*'s top-ranked stocks and using some of the other data provided, have added some input of their own. Among other suggestions, they advise sticking to companies ranked by *Value Line* in the top third of their industries, with high safety rankings and low debt ratios, with strong five-year growth in sales and earnings, and to companies at the low end of their historical price/earnings range. The Ladies also include a rather long list of recipes in their book. It is not known whether these have any effect on investment performance.

While there are obviously other effective investment methods, a reasonable question at this point would be: How does the idea of ferreting out investment winners from the stock market's hidden nooks and crannies stack up against the methods just discussed?

While certainly reasonable, this question may be a little misleading. Simply because you'll be looking for investments in out-of-the-way places doesn't mean that you can't or shouldn't apply some of the wisdom gleaned from studying the winning methods of a Graham, Buffett, or Lynch. Of course, once you've gone to the trouble of finding an interesting investment in a remote corner of the market, hopefully your analysis won't have to be any more subtle than figuring out whether an anvil fell on your head. Alas, although this is a worthy and not entirely unrealistic goal, life won't always be that easy.

Applying some lessons from the masters, at the very least, should help when the investment decisions become a bit more taxing. At most, since picking your spots is one of the keys to your success, following the basic principles of these investment greats should keep you focused in the right places.

THE SECRET HIDING PLACES
OF STOCK-MARKET PROFITS

All right, already. Where are these secret hiding places?

Don't worry. You don't have to look under Love Canal or get shot down spying over some secret Russian military base. It's not that straightforward. The answer is: stock-market profits can be hiding anywhere, and their hiding places are always changing. In fact, the underlying theme to most of these investment situations *is* change. Something out of the ordinary course of business is taking place that creates an investment opportunity. The list of corporate events that can result in big profits for you runs the gamut—spinoffs, mergers, restructurings, rights offerings, bankruptcies, liquidations, asset sales, distributions. And it's not just the events themselves that can provide profits; each such event can produce a whole host of new securities with their own extraordinary investment potential.

The great thing is, there's always *something* happening. Dozens of corporate events each week, too many for any one person to follow. But that's the point: you can't follow all of them, and you don't have to. Even finding one good opportunity a month is far more than you should need or want. As you read through this book, in example after example, in lesson after lesson, you may wonder "How the hell could I have found that one?" or "I never would have figured that out!" Both are probably true. But there will be plenty of others that you do find and can figure out. Even after you learn where to look for new ideas, the notion that you can cover even one-tenth of these special corporate events is a pipe dream. On the other hand, making incredible profits over your lifetime from the ones you do work on, isn't. The old cliché holds true: "Teach a man to fish. . . ."

What about all the other ways to get rich? There are no flaws in the investment methods of Warren Buffett or Peter Lynch. The problem is that you're not likely to be the next Buffett or Lynch. Investing in great businesses at good prices makes sense. Figuring out which are the great ones is the tough part. Monopoly newspapers and network broadcasters were once considered near-perfect businesses; then new forms of competition and the last recession brought those businesses a little bit closer to earth. The world is a complicated and competitive place. It is only getting more so. The challenges you face in choosing the few stellar businesses that will stand out in the future will be even harder than the ones faced by Buffett when he was building his fortune. Are you up to the task? Do you have to be?

Finding the next Wal-Mart, McDonald's, or Gap is also a

tough one. There are many more failures than successes. Using your own experiences and intuition to choose good investments is excellent advice. It should be applied in every investment you make. You *should* invest only in what you know and understand. It's just that Peter Lynch is an especially talented individual. It's likely that he knows and understands more than you when it comes down to making the tough calls.

On the other hand, Ben Graham's statistical approach was actually designed with the individual investor in mind. A widely diversified portfolio of stocks with low P/E ratios and low price-to-book ratios still produces excellent results and is relatively easy to emulate. Graham figured that if you owned twenty or thirty of these statistical bargains, you didn't need to do extensive research. You don't. Reading and studying Graham's work is how I first became fascinated with the stock market. I still apply his teachings wherever and whenever I can. It's just that if you are willing to do some of your own work, pick your spots, and look in places where others are not looking, you can do significantly better than Graham's more passive method.

Recently, it became even easier to do your own research. Information that in Graham's day wasn't available at all, or if it was, had to be uncovered from obscure state and federal filings, is now readily available. Until recently the same information, located among the prodigious amounts of public filings that companies are required to make with the SEC, was available but largely inaccessible. Documents describing the type of extraordinary corporate changes and events that will be the source of your investment profits were usually provided by private corporations charging up to $200 or $300 for one document. Now, this same information is instantly available on—you guessed it—the Internet, for the price of a phone call. Of course, you still have to be willing to read it.

Are there any drawbacks to investing in these special corporate situations? Two come immediately to mind. The first you know: it will take some work. The good news is that you will be well paid. The other drawback may or may not apply to you. Although some of these extraordinary corporate events play out over a period of years, others transpire over a period of months. Your investment advantage is usually at its greatest immediately before, during and right after the corporate event or change. Your window of opportunity may be short and therefore your holding period may also be short. As there is a tax advantage for many people from receiving long-term capital gains (from investments held more than one year), and an advantage for everyone in deferring their taxable gains by not selling appreciated securities, a short holding period in some of these situations creates a disadvantage compared to the long-term strategies of Buffett, Lynch, and Graham. Fortunately, you can avoid some of these disadvantages either by investing in only those situations that take several years to fully play out or by investing through your pension, IRA, or other retirement accounts. (Qualifying retirement accounts can generally be managed without concern for taxes.)

One more point: although most people take comfort in crowds, this is not where successful investors generally look for good investment ideas. Nevertheless, you may take comfort in the fact that the practice of investing in companies undergoing corporate change is not an alien concept to Buffett, Lynch, or Graham. Each of these great investors has spent some time investing in this arena. It's just that Graham was most concerned about passing on his wisdom to the individual investor; he felt accumulating a diversified portfolio of statistical bargains would be a more accessible way for most people to invest. Buffett and Lynch both had the problem of investing huge sums of money—billions of dollars. It is often difficult to take large enough positions in these special-investment situations to make an impact on that size portfolio. For your first quarter billion or so, though, it's no problem. (Call me when you get there.)

So roll up your sleeves and put your thinking caps on—you're going on a wild ride into the stock market's Twilight Zone. You'll go places where others fear to tread—or at least don't know about. When you enter these largely uncharted waters and discover the secrets buried there, you will finally know what it feels like to be one of the glorious few who climb Mount Everest, plant a flag at the North Pole, or walk on the moon. (Okay, okay—so it'll probably feel more like finishing a crossword puzzle. I've never done that either, but I'm sure that feels great, too!)

In any event, let's get going.

Chapter 3

Chips Off the Old Stock

Spinoffs, Partial Spinoffs, and Rights Offerings

I lost a bet. The stakes—dinner at Lutèce, loser treats. Being a bachelor at the time, my idea of living was to slap a slice of cheese on top of an uncut bagel (my own recipe—not one from the Beardstown Ladies). So, there I was, at perhaps the finest restaurant in the world, certainly in New York, looking over the menu. Over walks a gentleman in full chef's garb to help with our order. Somehow, his outfit didn't tip me off that this was actually Andre Soltner, proprietor and head chef.

Pointing to one of the appetizers on the menu, I asked innocently, "Is this one any good?"

"No, it stinks!" came Soltner's reply.

Even though he was just kidding around, I did get the point. Pretty much everything on the menu was going to be good. Selecting Lutèce was the important culinary decision, my particular menu choices were just fine tuning.

Keep this concept in mind as you read through the next several chapters. It's great to look for investments in places others are not, but it's not enough. You also have to look in the right places. If you preselect investment areas that put you ahead of the game even before you start (the "Lutèces" of the investment world), the most important work is already done. You'll still have plenty of decisions to make, but if you're picking and choosing your spots from an already outstanding menu, your choices are less likely to result in indigestion.

SPINOFFS

The first investment area we'll visit is surprisingly unappetizing. It's an area of discarded corporate refuse usually referred to as "spinoffs." Spinoffs can take many forms but the end result is usually the same: A corporation takes a subsidiary, division, or part of its business and separates it from the parent company by creating a new, independent, freestanding company. In most cases, shares of the new "spinoff" company are distributed or sold to the parent company's existing shareholders.

There are plenty of reasons why a company might choose to unload or otherwise separate itself from the fortunes of the business to be spun off. There is really only one reason to pay attention when they do: you can make a pile of money investing in spinoffs. The facts are overwhelming. Stocks of spinoff companies, and even shares of the parent companies that do the spinning off, significantly and consistently outperform the market averages.

One study completed at Penn State, covering a twenty-five-year period ending in 1988, found that stocks of spinoff companies outperformed their industry peers and the Standard & Poor's 500 by about 10 percent *per year* in their first three- years of independence.* The parent companies also managed to do pretty well—outperforming the companies in their industry by more than 6 percent annually during the same three-year period. Other studies have reached similarly promising conclusions about the prospects for spinoff companies.

What can these results mean for you? If you accept the assumption that over long periods of time the market averages a return of approximately 10 percent per year, then, theoretically, outperforming the market by 10 percent could have you earning 20-percent annual returns. If the past experience of these studies holds true in the future, spectacular results could be achieved merely by buying a portfolio of recently spun-off companies. Translation: 20-percent annual returns—no special talents or utensils required.

But what happens if you're willing to do a little of your own work? Picking your favorite spinoff situations—not merely buying every spinoff or a random sampling—should result in annual returns even better than 20 percent. Pretty significant, considering that Warren Buffett, everyone's favorite billionaire, has only managed to eke out 28 percent annually (albeit over forty years). Is it possible that just by picking your

* Patrick J. Cusatis, James A. Miles, and J. Randall Woolridge, "Restructuring Through Spinoffs," *Journal of Financial Economics* 33 (1993).

spots within the spinoff area, you could achieve results rivaling those of an investment great like Buffett?

Nah, you say. Something's wrong here. First of all, who's to say that spinoffs will continue to perform as well in the future as they have in the past? Second, when everyone finds out that spinoffs produce these extraordinary returns, won't the prices of spinoff shares be bid up to the point where the extra returns disappear? And finally—about these results even greater than 20 percent—why should you have an edge in figuring out which spinoffs have the greatest chance for outsize success?

O ye of little faith. Of course spinoffs will continue to outperform the market averages—and yes, even after more people find out about their sensational record. As for why you'll have a great shot at picking the really big winners—that's an easy one—you'll be able to because I'll show you how. To understand the how's and the why's, let's start with the basics.

Why do companies pursue spinoff transactions in the first place? Usually the reasoning behind a spinoff is fairly straightforward:

> ▪ **Unrelated businesses may be separated via a spinoff transaction so that the separate businesses can be better appreciated by the market.**
>
> For example, a conglomerate in the steel and insurance business can spin off one of the businesses and create an investment attractive to people who want to invest in either insurance or steel but not both.
>
> Of course, before a spinoff, some insurance investors might still have an interest in buying stock in the conglom-

erate, but most likely only at a discount (reflecting the "forced" purchase of an unwanted steel business).

■ **Sometimes, the motivation for a spinoff comes from a desire to separate out a "bad" business so that an unfettered "good" business can show through to investors.**
This situation (as well as the previous case of two unrelated businesses) may also prove a boon to management. The "bad" business may be an undue drain on management time and focus. As separate companies, a focused management group for each entity has a better chance of being effective.

■ **Sometimes a spinoff is a way to get value to shareholders for a business that can't be easily sold.**
Occasionally, a business is such a dog that its parent company can't find a buyer at a reasonable price. If the spinoff is merely in an unpopular business that still earns some money, the parent may load the new spinoff with debt. In this way, debt is shifted from the parent to the new spinoff company (creating more value for the parent).

On the other hand, a really awful business may actually receive additional capital from the parent—just so the spinoff can survive on its own and the parent can be rid of it.

■ **Tax considerations can also influence a decision to pursue a spinoff instead of an outright sale.**
If a business with a low tax basis is to be divested, a spinoff may be the most lucrative way to achieve value for shareholders. If certain IRS criteria are met, a spinoff can qualify

as a tax-free transaction—neither the corporation nor the individual stockholders incur a tax liability upon distribution of the spinoff shares.

A cash sale of the same division or subsidiary with the proceeds dividended out to shareholders would, in most cases, result in both a taxable gain to the corporation and a taxable dividend to shareholders.

■ **A spinoff may solve a strategic, antitrust, or regulatory issue, paving the way for other transactions or objectives.** In a takeover, sometimes the acquirer doesn't want to, or can't for regulatory reasons, buy one of the target company's businesses. A spinoff of that business to the target company's shareholders prior to the merger is often a solution.

In some cases, a bank or insurance subsidiary may subject the parent company or the subsidiary to unwanted regulations. A spinoff of the regulated entity can solve this problem.

The list could go on. It is interesting to note, however, that regardless of the initial motivation behind a spinoff transaction, newly spun-off companies tend to handily outperform the market. Why should this be? Why should it continue?

Luckily for you, the answer is that these extra spinoff profits are practically built into the system. The spinoff process itself is a fundamentally inefficient method of distributing stock to the wrong people. Generally, the new spinoff stock isn't sold, it's given to shareholders who, for the most part, were investing in the parent company's business. Therefore, once the spinoff's shares are distributed to the parent company's shareholders, they are typically sold immediately without regard to price or fundamental value.

The initial excess supply has a predictable effect on the spinoff stock's price: it is usually depressed. Supposedly shrewd institutional investors also join in the selling. Most of the time spinoff companies are much smaller than the parent company. A spinoff may be only 10 or 20 percent the size of the parent. Even if a pension or mutual fund took the time to analyze the spinoff's business, often the size of these companies is too small for an institutional portfolio, which only contains companies with much larger market capitalizations.

Many funds can only own shares of companies that are included in the Standard & Poor's 500 index, an index that includes only the country's largest companies. If an S&P 500 company spins off a division, you can be pretty sure that right out of the box that division will be the subject of a huge amount of indiscriminate selling. Does this practice seem foolish? Yes. Understandable? Sort of. Is it an opportunity for you to pick up some low-priced shares? Definitely.

Another reason spinoffs do so well is that capitalism, with all its drawbacks, actually works. When a business and its management are freed from a large corporate parent, pent-up entrepreneurial forces are unleashed. The combination of accountability, responsibility, and more direct incentives take their natural course. After a spinoff, stock options, whether issued by the spinoff company or the parent, can more directly compensate the managements of each business. Both the spinoff and the parent company benefit from this reward system.

In the Penn State study, the largest stock gains for spinoff companies took place not in the first year after the spinoff but in the second. It may be that it takes a full year for the initial selling pressure to wear off before a spinoff's stock can perform at its best. More likely, though, it's not until the year after a spinoff that many of the entrepreneurial changes and initiatives can kick in and begin to be recognized by the marketplace. Whatever the reason for this exceptional second-year performance, the results do seem to indicate that when it comes to spinoffs, there is more than enough time to do research and make profitable investments.

One last thought on why the spinoff process seems to yield such successful results for shareholders of the spinoff company and the parent: in most cases, if you examine the motivation behind a decision to pursue a spinoff, it boils down to a desire on the part of management and a company's board of directors to increase shareholder value. Of course, since this is their job and primary responsibility, theoretically all management and board decisions should be based on this principle. Although that's the way it should be, it doesn't always work that way.

It may be human nature or the American way or the natural order of things, but most managers and boards have traditionally sought to expand their empire, domain, or sphere of influence, not contract it. Perhaps that's why there are so many mergers and acquisitions and why so many, especially those outside of a company's core competence, fail. Maybe that's why many businesses (airlines and retailers come to mind) continually expand, even when it might be better to return excess cash to shareholders. The motives for the acquisition or expansion may be confused in the first place. However, this is rarely the case with a spinoff. Assets are being shed and influence lost, all with the hope that shareholders will be better off after the separation.

It is ironic that the architects of a failed acquistion may well end up using the spinoff technique to bail themselves out. Hopefully, the choice of a spinoff is an indication that a degree of discipline and shareholder orientation has returned. In any case, a strategy of investing in the shares of a spinoff or parent company should ordinarily result in a pre-selected portfolio of strongly shareholder-focused companies.

CHOOSING THE BEST OF THE BEST

Once you're convinced that spinoff stocks are an attractive hunting ground for stock-market profits, the next thing you'll want to know is, how can you tilt the odds even more in your favor? What are the attributes and circumstances that suggest one spinoff may outperform another? What do you look for and how hard is it to figure out?

You don't need special formulas or mathematical models to help you choose the really big winners. Logic, common sense, and a little experience are all that's required. That may sound trite but it is nevertheless true. Most professional investors don't even think about individual spinoff situations. Either they have too many companies to follow, or they can only invest in companies of a certain type or size, or they just can't go to the trouble of analyzing extraordinary corporate events. As a consequence, just doing a little of your own thinking about each spinoff opportunity can give you a very large edge.

Hard to believe? Let's review some examples to see what I mean.

CASE STUDY

HOST MARRIOTT/
MARRIOTT INTERNATIONAL

During the 1980s, Marriott Corporation aggressively expanded its empire by building a large number of hotels. However, the cream of their business was not owning hotels, but charging management fees for managing hotels owned by others. Their strategy, which had been largely successful, was to build hotels, sell them, but keep the lucrative management contracts for those same hotels. When everything in the real-estate market hit the fan in the early 1990s, Marriott was stuck with a load of unsalable hotels in an overbuilt market and burdened with the billions in debt it had taken on to build the hotels.

Enter Stephen Bollenbach, financial whiz, with a great idea. Bollenbach, fresh from helping Donald Trump turn around his gambling empire, and then chief financial officer at Marriott (now CEO of Hilton), figured a way out for Marriott. The financial covenants in Marriott's publicly traded debt allowed (or rather, did not prohibit) the spinning off of Marriott's lucrative management-contracts business, which had a huge income stream but very few hard assets. Bollenbach's concept was to leave all of the unsalable hotel properties and the low-growth concession business — burdened with essentially all of the company's debt — in one company, Host Marriott, and spin off the highly desirable management-service business, more or less debt free, into a company to be called Marriott International.

According to the plan, Bollenbach would become the new chief executive of Host Marriott. Further, Marriott International (the "good" Marriott) would be required to extend to Host Marriott a $600-million line of credit to help with any liquidity needs and the Marriott family, owners of 25 percent of the combined Marriott Corporation, would continue to own 25-percent stakes in both Marriott International and Host. The spinoff transaction was scheduled to be consummated some time in the middle of 1993.

Keep in mind, no extensive research was required to learn all this. *The Wall Street Journal* (and many other major newspapers) laid out all this background information for me when Marriott first announced the split-up in October 1992. It didn't take more than reading this basic scenario in the newspapers, though, to get me very excited. After all, here was a case where in one fell swoop an apparently excellent hotel-management business was finally going to shed billions in debt and a pile of tough-to-sell real estate. Of course, as a result of the transaction creating this new powerhouse, Marriott International, there would be some "toxic waste." A company would be left, Host Marriott, that retained this unwanted real estate and billions in debt.

Obviously, I was excited about . . . the toxic waste. "Who the hell is gonna want to own this thing?" was the way my thinking went. No institution, no individual, nobody and their mother would possibly hold onto the newly created Host Marriott after the spinoff took place. The selling pressure would be tremendous. I'd be the only one around scooping up the bargain-priced stock.

Now, almost anyone you talk to about investing will say that he is a *contrarian*, meaning he goes against the crowd and conventional thinking. Clearly, by definition, *everyone* can't be a contrarian. That being said . . . I'm a contrarian. That doesn't mean I'll jump in front of a speeding Mack truck, just because nobody else in the crowd will. It means that if I've thought through an issue I try to follow my own opinion even when the crowd thinks differently.

The fact that everyone was going to be selling Host Marriott after the spinoff didn't, by itself, mean that the stock would be a great contrarian buy. The crowd, after all, could be right. Host Marriott could be just what it looked like: a speeding Mack truck loaded down with unsalable real estate and crushing debt. On the other hand, there were a few things about this situation beyond its obvious contrarian appeal (it looked awful) that made me willing, even excited, to look a bit further.

In fact, Host Marriott had a number of characteristics that I look for when trying to choose a standout spinoff opportunity.

1. INSTITUTIONS DON'T WANT IT (AND THEIR REASONS DON'T INVOLVE THE INVESTMENT MERITS).

There were several reasons why institutional portfolio managers or pension funds wouldn't want to own Host Marriott. We've already covered the issue of huge debt and unpopular real-estate assets. These arguments go to the investment merits and might be very valid reasons not to own Host. However, after the announcement of the transaction in October 1992 only a small portion of the facts about Host Marriott had been disclosed. How informed could an investment judgment at this early stage really be?

From the initial newspaper accounts, though, Host looked so awful that *most institutions would be discouraged from doing any further research on the new stock.* Since a huge amount of information and disclosure was sure to become available before the spinoff's fruition (estimated to be in about nine months), I vowed to read it—first, to see if Host was going to be as bad as it looked and second, because I figured almost nobody else would.

Another reason why institutions weren't going to be too hot to own Host was its size. Once again, not exactly the investment merits. According to analysts quoted in the initial newspaper reports, Host would account for only about 10 or 15 percent of the total value being distributed to shareholders, with the rest of the value attributable to the "good" business, Marriott International. A leveraged (highly indebted) stock with a total market capitalization only a fraction of the original $2 billion Marriott Corporation was probably not going to be an appropriate size for most of Marriott's original holders.

Also, Host was clearly in a different business than most institutional investors had been seeking to invest in when they bought their Marriott shares. Host was going to own hotels; whereas the business that attracted most Marriott investors was hotel management. Though owning commercial real estate and hotels can be a good business, the Marriott group of shareholders, for the most part, had other interests and were likely to sell their Host shares. Sales of stock solely for this reason would not be based on the specific investment merits and therefore, might create a buying opportunity.

(*Note*: For reasons unique to the Marriott case, the spin-off was actually considered, at least technically, to be Marriott International—even though its stock would represent the vast majority of the value of the combined entities. For purposes of this illustration (and for the purposes of being accurate in every sense other than technical), it will be more helpful to think of Host—the entitity comprising 10 to 15 percent of Marriott's original stock market valuation—as the spinoff.)

2. INSIDERS WANT IT.

Insider participation is one of the key areas to look for when picking and choosing between spinoffs—for me, the *most* important area. Are the managers of the new spinoff incentivized along the same lines as shareholders? Will they receive a large part of their potential compensation in stock, restricted stock, or options? Is there a plan for them to acquire more? When all the required public documents about the spinoff have been filed, I usually look at this area first.

In the case of Host Marriott, something from the initial press reports caught my eye. Stephen Bollenbach, the architect of the plan, was to become Host's chief executive. Of course, as the paper reported, he had just helped Donald Trump turn around his troubled hotel and gambling empire. In that respect, he seemed a fine candidate for the job. One thing bothered me, though: It didn't make sense that the man responsible for successfully saving a sinking ship—by figuring out a way to throw all that troubled real estate and burdensome debt overboard—should voluntarily jump the now secured ship into a sinking lifeboat, Host Marriott.

"Great idea, Bollenbach!" the story would have to go. "I think you've really saved us! Now, when you're done throwing that real estate and debt overboard, why don't you toss yourself over the side as well! Pip, pip. Use that wobbly lifeboat if you want. Cheerio!"

It could have happened that way. More likely, I thought, Host might not be a hopeless basket case and Bollenbach was going to be well incentivized to make the new company work. I vowed to check up on his compensation package when the SEC documents were filed. The more stock incentive, the better. Additionally, the Marriott family was still going to own 25 percent of Host after the spinoff. Although the chief reason for the deal was to free up Marriott International from its debt and real estate burden, after the spinoff was completed it would still be to the family's benefit to have the stock of Host Marriott thrive.

3. A PREVIOUSLY HIDDEN INVESTMENT OPPORTUNITY IS CREATED OR REVEALED.

This could mean that a great business or a statistically cheap stock is uncovered as a result of the spinoff. In the case of Host, though, I noticed a different kind of opportunity: tremendous leverage.

If the analysts quoted in the original press reports turned out to be correct, Host stock could trade at $3–5 per share but the new company would also have somewhere between $20–25 per share in debt. For purposes of our example, let's assume the equity in Host would have a market value of $5 per share and the debt per Host share would be $25. That would make the approximate value of all the assets in Host $30. Thus a 15 percent move up in the value of Host's assets could practically double the stock (.15 × $30 = $4.50). Great work if you can get it. What about a 15-percent move down in value? Don't ask.

I doubted, however, that Host Marriott would be structured to sink into oblivion—at least not immediately. I knew that all the new Host shareholders had good reason to dump their toxic waste on the market as soon as possible. With the prospect of liability and lawsuits from creditors, employees, and shareholders, though, I suspected that a quick demise of Host Marriott, the corporation, was not part of the plan. Add to this the facts that Marriott International, the "good" company, would be on the hook to lend Host up to $600 million, the Marriott family would still own 25 percent of Host, and Bollenbach would be heading up the new company—it seemed in everyone's best interest for Host Marriott to survive and hopefully thrive. At the very least, after I did some more work, it seemed likely that with such a leveraged payoff it had the makings of an exciting bet.

Believe it or not, far from being a one-time insight, tremendous leverage is an attribute found in many spinoff situations. Remember, one of the primary reasons a corporation may choose to spin off a particular business is its desire to receive value for a business it deems undesirable and troublesome to sell. What better way to extract value from a spinoff than to palm off some of the parent company's debt onto the spinoff's balance sheet? Every dollar of debt transferred to the new spinoff company adds a dollar of value to the parent.

The result of this process is the creation of a large number of inordinately leveraged spinoffs. Though the market may value the equity in one of these spinoffs at $1 per every $5, $6, or even $10 of corporate debt in the newly created spin-off, $1 is also the amount of *your* maximum loss. Individual investors are not responsible for the debts of a corporation. Say what you will about the risks of investing in such companies, the rewards of sound reasoning and good research are vastly multiplied when applied in these leveraged circumstances.

In case you haven't been paying attention, we've just managed to build a very viable investment thesis or rationale for investing in Host Marriott stock. To review, Host could turn out to be a good pick because:

- Most sane institutional investors were going to sell their Host Marriott stock *before* looking at it, which would, hopefully, create a bargain price.

- Key insiders, subject to more research, appeared to have a vested interest in Host's success, and

- Tremendous leverage would magnify our returns if Host turned out, for some reason, to be more attractive than its initial appearances indicated.

If events went our way, with any luck these attributes would help us do even better than the average spinoff.

So, how did things work out? As expected (and hoped), many institutions managed to sell their Host stock at a low price. Insiders, according to the SEC filings, certainly ended up with a big vested interest, as nearly 20 percent of the new company's stock was made available for management and employee incentives. Finally, Host's debt situation, a turn-off for most people—though a potential opportunity for us—turned out to be structured much more attractively than it appeared from just reading the initial newspaper accounts.

So, how'd it work out? Pretty well, I think. Host Marriott stock (a.k.a. the "toxic waste") nearly tripled within four months of the spinoff. Extraordinary results from looking at a situation that practically everyone else gave up on.

Are *you* ready to give up? Too much thinking? Too much work? Can't be bothered with all those potential profits? Or, maybe, just maybe, you'd like to learn a little bit more.

DIGGING FOR BURIED TREASURE

So far the only work we've really discussed has been reading about a potentially interesting situation in the newspaper. Now (you knew there was a catch), it gets a bit more involved. You're about to be sent off on a mind-numbing journey into the arcane world of investment research, complete with multi-hundred-page corporate documents and mountains of Securities and Exchange Commission (SEC) filings.

Before you panic, take a deep breath. There's no need to quit your day job. Sure there will be some work to do—a little sleuthing here, some reading over there—but nothing too taxing. Just think of it as digging for buried treasure. Nobody thinks about the actual digging—insert shovel, step on shovel, fling dirt over shoulder—when a little treasure is on the line. When you're "digging" with an exciting goal in sight, the nature of the task changes completely. The same thinking applies here.

Essentially, it all boils down to a simple two-step process. First, identify where you think the treasure (or in our case the profit opportunity) lies. Second, after you've identified the spot (preferably marked by a big red X), then, and only then, start digging. No sense (and no fun) digging up the whole neighborhood.

So at last you're ready to go. You're prospecting in a lucrative area: spinoffs. You have a plausible investment thesis, one that may help you do even better than the average spinoff. Now, it's time to roll up your sleeves and do a little investigative work. Right? Well, that is right—only not so fast.

In the Marriott example, the spinoff plan was originally announced in October 1992. Although the deal garnered plenty of press coverage over the ensuing months, the relevant SEC filings were not available until June and July 1993. The actual spinoff didn't take place until the end of September—nearly a year after initial disclosure. While six to nine months is a more usual time frame, in some cases the process can stretch to over a year.

If you have an impatient nature and are partial to fast action, waiting around for spinoffs to play out fully may not be for you. Horse racing never succeeded in Las Vegas because most gamblers couldn't wait the two minutes it took to lose their money. The same outcome, only more immediate, was available in too many other places.

The financial markets have also been known to accommodate those who prefer instant gratification. On the other hand, having the time to think and do research at your own pace and convenience without worrying about the latest in communication technologies has obvious advantages for the average nonprofessional investor. Besides, once you've spent a year prospecting in *The Wall Street Journal* (or in countless other business publications) for interesting spinoff opportunities, there should, at any given time, be at least one or two previously announced and now imminent spinoffs ripe for further research and possible investment.

As a matter of fact, here comes another one now.

CASE STUDY

STRATTEC SECURITY/
BRIGGS & STRATTON

In May of 1994, Briggs & Stratton, a manufacturer of small gas-powered engines (used mostly in outdoor power equipment), announced its intention to spin off its automotive-lock division. The spinoff was slated to take place in late 1994 or early in 1995. The automotive-lock division (later to be named Strattec Security) was a small division representing less than 10 percent of Briggs & Stratton's total sales and earnings.

Since Briggs, the parent company, was included in the S&P 500 average with a market capitalization of $1 billion, it seemed that Strattec might turn out to be a prime candidate for institutional selling once its shares were distributed to Briggs shareholders. Not only was manufacturing locks for cars and trucks unrelated to Briggs's small-engine business, but it appeared that Strattec would have a market value of under $100 million—a size completely inappropriate for most of Briggs & Stratton's institutional shareholders.

Although Strattec had the makings of a classic spinoff opportunity, it stayed on the back burner until November 1994 when something called an SEC Form 10 was publicly filed. In general, this is the public filing that contains most of the pertinent information about a new spinoff company. A Form 10 is filed in cases where the new spinoff represents a small piece of the parent company; smaller transactions do not require a shareholder vote. In cases where the spinoff represents a major portion of a parent company's assets, a proxy document is prepared so that shareholders can vote on the proposed split-up. In those cases, the proxy contains most of the same information found in the Form 10. (Don't worry about taking notes now. How to go about obtaining these various filings and proxies will be well covered in chapter 7.)

Not until January 1995, however, when an amended Form 10 was filed, filling in some of the details and blanks left in the original filing, was it really time to do some work. According to this document, the spinoff was scheduled to be distributed on February 27. As my first move with any of these filings is to check out what the insiders—key management and/or controlling shareholders—are up to, it was nice to see part of the answer right on the first page following the introduction. Under the heading "Reasons for the Distribution," the Board of Directors of Briggs revealed the primary reason for the spinoff. The Board's motives were classic: to "provide incentive compensation to its key employees that is equity-based and tied to the value of [Strattec's] business operations and performance as a separately traded public company, not as an indistinguishable unit of Briggs."

According to this section of the document, a Stock Incentive Plan granting various stock awards to officers and key employees would reserve over 12 percent of the new company's shares to provide incentives for employees. While this amount of stock incentive may seem generous to an outside observer, as far as I am concerned the more generous a Board is with its compensation plans, the better—as long as this generosity takes the form of stock option or restricted stock plans.

In fact, a theme common to many attractive investment situations is that management and employees have been incentivized to act like owners. Investors might well be better

77

off if the law actually granted top executives and key personnel a minimum ownership stake in their employer. As this sort of government intervention is probably as unlikely as it is unwise, you can accomplish much the same result by sticking to investments in companies like Strattec, where management can prosper only alongside shareholders.

In addition to checking up on the insiders, it usually pays to spend some time on the first few pages of any Form 10, proxy, or similar document. These pages usually contain a detailed table of contents, followed by a five- or eight-page summary of the next hundred or more pages. Here is where you can pinpoint areas of interest and choose where to focus your efforts selectively. Frankly, reruns of *Gilligan's Island* hold more appeal than a page-by-page read-through of an entire proxy or Form 10—so selectivity is key. Not only do these documents have entire sections disclosing the various economic interests of insiders but, importantly, somewhere amid all the verbiage are the pro-forma income statements and balance sheets for the new spinoff. (Pro-forma statements show what the balance sheet and income statement would have looked like if the new entity had existed as an independent company in prior years.)

According to the pro-forma income statement found in the summary section of the Form 10, earnings for Strattec's fiscal year ending in June 1994 came in at $1.18 per share. Excluding some one-time expenses, earnings for the more recent six-month period, ended December 1994, looked to be up a further 10 percent from the same period in 1993.

Armed with this limited information, I tried to take a stab at what a fair price for Strattec might be when it finally started trading at the end of February 1995.

As primarily a manufacturer of locks and keys for new automobiles and trucks, Strattec, according to logic and the Form 10, fell under the category of original-equipment manufacturer (OEM) for the automobile industry. The next logical step was to find out at what price most other companies in the same industry traded relative to their earnings. Very simply, if all the OEM suppliers to the auto industry traded at a price equal to 10 times their annual earnings (i.e., at a price/earnings ratio or P/E of 10), then a fair price for Strattec might end up being $11.80 per share ($1.18 multiplied by 10).

Later in the book, we will cover several reference sources that provide the type of data we will need to do our comparative pricing. In this case, I used *Value Line*, as it is generally readily available and easy to use. *Value Line*'s contents are organized according to industry groups. Under the grouping, "Auto Parts (Original Equipment)," I was able to determine that a range of roughly 9 to 13 times earnings was a reasonable range for P/E's within Strattec's industry group. That meant that a reasonable price range for Strattec might be somewhere between $10.62 per share ($1.18 × 9) and approximately $15.34 ($1.18 × 13). If I wanted to be more aggressive, since Strattec's earnings had grown approximately 10 percent in the six months since the year ended in June 1994, a range maybe 10 percent higher might be appropriate.

While all of this analysis was fine and dandy, unless Strattec started trading at $6 or $7 a share due to intense selling pressure, I wasn't going to get rich from anything discussed so far. Further, I didn't know much about Strattec's industry, but I did know one thing. Supplying parts to auto manufacturers is generally considered to be a crappy business. Certainly if I did decide to buy stock in Strattec, Warren Buffett was not going to be my competition. (Actually, as a general rule, Buffett won't even consider individual investments of less than $100 million; here the entire company was going to be valued at less than $100 million.)

The interesting part came when I was reading the few pages listed under the heading of "Business of the Company." This was not hard to find. It turned out that Strattec was by far the largest supplier of locks to General Motors, and that this business represented about 50 percent of Strattec's sales. Strattec also provided almost all of Chrysler's locks, and this business totaled over 16 percent of Strattec's total revenues. From this, I guessed that Strattec must be pretty good at making car locks. The next piece of information, though, got me very interested.

According to its filing, "based upon current product commitments, the Company [Strattec] believes Ford will become its second-largest customer during fiscal 1996 [year ended June 1996], if such commitments are fulfilled as expected." This section didn't feature banner headlines like the *Wham!*, *Socko!* and *Blamo!* from the old Batman T.V. show—but it had almost the same impact on me. Since all of the revenue and earnings numbers discussed so far didn't include any Ford business, a new customer expected to order more locks than needed by the entire Chrysler Corporation was pretty big news.

As Chrysler was currently Strattec's second-biggest customer, accounting for over 16 percent of total sales, it made sense that for Ford to take over second place, its new business had to represent even more than 16 percent. (Since GM was the biggest customer with about 50 percent of Strattec's sales, it also meant that Ford's business had to be less than this amount.) In short, here was a very interesting piece of information that should substantially increase the value of Strattec's business. My hope was that this information would not be reflected in Strattec's stock price until I was able to make some bargain purchases.

From a qualitative standpoint, there was something else about Strattec's business that seemed attractive. Strattec was by far the biggest factor in the automotive lock market. With a majority of General Motors's business and all of Chrysler's, Strattec seemed to have a very strong niche. So, too, the addition of Ford's business meant that the quality and price of Strattec's products must be headed in the right direction. I figured most of the other OEM suppliers being used for comparison purposes were unlikely to have a better market position than Strattec. All of this combined meant that a P/E multiple for Strattec at the higher end of the industry range might be appropriate.

Of course, I had no intention of buying my stock at the

top end of the industry P/E range, justified or not. However, if it were possible to buy Strattec at the low end of industry valuations (nine times earnings or so), without taking into account the new Ford business, *that* might be a very attractive investment.

The outcome? For several months after Strattec began trading, the stock traded freely between 10½ and 12. This was clearly at the low end of the industry range—before taking into account (1) the Ford business, (2) Strattec's far better than average market niche, and (3) the recent 10 percent profit increase during the most recent six months. In short, it was easy to buy shares in Strattec at a very attractive price. This was confirmed as Strattec traded to $18 per share before the end of 1995—a 50 percent plus gain in less than eight months. Not too bad—and fortunately, far from an unusual spinoff opportunity.

Okay, I know what you're thinking. The money's all fine and good—but auto parts—sheesh—they're so darn boring! No problem. You *can* have it all—money and excitement—because our next stop is the wonderful world of home shopping!

HOME SHOPPING BONANZA—THE CARTWRIGHTS WERE NEVER THIS RICH

I didn't think my trip into the world of home shopping was going to be that exciting. Of course, every third trip flipping through the cable box, like everybody else I would catch a glimpse of a porcelain dog or some other useless item. As my house is filled with ridiculous gizmos and gadgets—most hidden from view for face-saving reasons—and I wasn't a customer, I really had no idea who was buying this stuff. Because the stock had been a notorious high flyer in the 1980s and I routinely flipped past its channel, I never considered the Home Shopping Network as a potential investment situation.

An article that appeared in the premiere issue of *Smart Money* magazine in April 1992 changed that. In an article entitled "10 Stocks for the '90s," one of the ten choices turned out to be the Home Shopping Network. The basic premise of the article was that by studying the attributes of the biggest winners of the 1980s—by examining what they looked like back in 1980—a list of winners for the '90s could be compiled. There were several reasons why one of the choices, the Home Shopping Network, caught my eye.

First, most of the selection criteria for making the top-ten list involved Ben Graham's value measures (low price-to-earnings and/or cash-flow ratio, low price-to-book-value ratio, etc.). It was a surprise that a former high flyer like Home Shopping Network had fallen far enough to be considered a value stock. Second, Home Shopping's stock was priced just over $5 per share. While a single-digit stock price, in and of itself, should be meaningless, many institutions don't like to buy stocks priced under $10. Since in the United States most companies like their stocks to trade between $10 per share and $100, a stock that trades below $10 has, in many instances, fallen from grace. Due to a lower market capitalization at these prices, or the fact that stocks that have fallen from a higher price are inherently unpopular, opportunities can often be found in single-digit stocks as they are prone to be underanalyzed, underowned, and consequently mispriced.

The final reason Home Shopping Network looked to have potential was that—surprise, surprise—a spinoff was involved. (That's why we're here in the first place, remember?) According to the article, Home Shopping had plans to spin off its broadcast properties "to improve the quality of earnings." What this meant, I would find out later. It certainly looked like both the parent company, Home Shopping Network, and the spinoff, Silver King Communications, were worth some more study.

According to the Form 10, filed in August 1992, under the heading "Reasons for the Distribution," Home Shopping's management stated:

[M]anagement believes that the financial and investment communities do not fully understand how to value HSN [Home Shopping Network], in part because HSN is both a retail-oriented company and a broadcast company. Broadcast companies are typically valued based on cash flow while retail companies are typically valued on an earnings-per-share basis. The categorization of HSN as either a broadcast concern or a retail-oriented company results in the application of a single valuation methodology when a combination of the two valuation methods would be more appropriate. For instance, the valuation of

HSN's retail business and, likewise, the valuation of HSN as a retail-oriented business is severely discounted by the impact of the substantial depreciation and amortization costs associated with the broadcast assets of the Stations. HSN's Board of Directors believes that the separation of HSN and the (broadcast) Company would allow potential investors to more clearly understand the business of each company and may serve to attract increased investor interest in, and analyst coverage of, each company.

It turned out that Home Shopping Network had purchased twelve independent UHF television broadcast stations during the 1980s in an effort to expand the reach of its home-shopping program. According to the SEC filing, these stations reached approximately 27.5 million housholds representing "one of the largest audience reaches of any owned and operated, independent television broadcasting group in the United States." The only problem was, HSN had paid a lot of money for these stations. That wasn't so bad, but television stations don't have much in the way of assets. Their value derives from the cash stream received from advertising revenues (in Home Shopping's case, one never-ending commercial), not from the amount of broadcasting equipment used to transmit the program.

Unfortunately, paying a large purchase price for something that relies on a relatively small amount of fixed assets and working capital to generate profits usually results in a large amount of goodwill being placed on the balance sheet of the purchaser. Goodwill arises when the purchase price exceeds the value of the acquired company's identifiable assets (i.e., assets that can be identified—like broadcast equipment, receivables, and programming rights). This excess in purchase price over the value of these identifiable assets must be amortized (an expense similar to the depreciation charge for plant and equipment) over a period of years. Like depreciation, amortization of goodwill is a noncash expense that is deducted from reported earnings. (See chapter 7 for a full explanation of these terms.)

Since a broadcast property is the classic example of a business whose value is not closely tied to the amount of assets employed, broadcasters are generally valued on their cash flow (which adds back the noncash charges of depreciation and amortization to earnings), not on their reported earnings. Retailers, on the other hand, are valued based on their earnings. Home Shopping's SEC filing stated that figuring out the proper earnings multiple (P/E ratio) for the combined businesses was very difficult. According to the filing, the retail business should be valued based on a multiple of earnings, the broadcaster on a multiple of cash flow.

A quick look at Silver King's income statement highlighted this point very clearly. Silver King's operating earnings were slightly over $4 million for the most recent year. Its cash flow, however, totaled over $26 million ($4 million in operating earnings plus roughly $22 million of depreciation and amortization). Since broadcast equipment doesn't have to be replaced that often, capital spending on new plant and equipment was only about $3 million. This meant that, before accounting for interest and taxes, Silver King was actually earning nearly $23 million in cash from its operations: operating earnings of $4 million plus depreciation and amortization of $22 million, less $3 million in capital spending. (If you're a little lost, feel free to check out the cash-flow section of chapter 7.)

Of course, you wouldn't know that Home Shopping's broadcast division was such a big cash generator merely from looking at earnings. The broadcast properties contributed only $4 million to operating earnings, but as we've already seen, they added over $26 million to Home Shopping's operating cash flow. Since HSN had over 88 million shares outstanding, $4 million amounted to only about 4.5 cents per share of operating earnings lost from spinning off the entire broadcast division. But, wait, that's not the whole story.

Home Shopping, according to the SEC filings, was going to shift more than $140 million of debt over to Silver King as part of the spinoff process. At an interest rate of 9 percent, this meant that HSN was going to be relieved of over $12.6 million in annual interest costs (.09 × $140 million). The bottom line was that as far as much of Wall Street was concerned, the Home Shopping Network would earn more without the broadcast properties than with them! (Reported earnings before taxes would be approximately $8.6 million higher after the spinoff—$12.6 million less of interest expense, now on Silver King's books, while forgoing only $4 million in operating income by spinning off Silver King.)

Of course, given the huge cash-generating ability of HSN's TV stations, this wasn't the right way to look at things. But that was Home Shopping's point. They believed that investors were not including the value of the TV stations in HSN's price. In fact, considering the debt load taken on to buy the stations, investors may have been subtracting for them. (Since HSN borrowed heavily to buy the stations, investors may have subtracted the high interest costs from the stock's value—while only giving credit for the $4 million of operating income, not for the full cash flow.)

The whole situation had opportunity written all over it. Clearly, Silver King had the makings of an underfollowed and misunderstood spinoff situation. Silver King was going to have over $140 million of debt on its balance sheet. The value of the spinoff was going to be small relative to the value of each shareholder's stake in Home Shopping—hopefully making it inappropriate or unimportant to the shareholders receiving it. (The terms of the spinoff called for a one-for-ten distribution—meaning for every ten shares an investor held in Home Shopping Network, he or she would receive a distribution of only one share of Silver King Communications.) Moreover, Silver King was in a different business—broadcasting—than the retail business originally favored by the parent company's shareholders. And, perhaps most important, Silver King was earning a ton of cash that most of Home Shopping's shareholders, the ones receiving Silver King's shares, were unlikely to know about.

The investment opportunities didn't end there. The parent company, Home Shopping Network, was also worth a look. Since an investor who purchased HSN's stock based on reported earnings was probably not placing much value on the broadcast properties, maybe HSN stock wouldn't go down much after the spinoff. If that happened, the combined value of HSN and the spinoff could be more than the pre-spinoff price of HSN. It was even possible that, since Home Shopping's reported earnings would actually go up as a result of the spinoff, HSN's stock could trade higher without the broadcast properties than with them.

Before we get to the outcome, one more quick point. Whenever a parent company announces the spinoff of a division engaged in a highly regulated industry (like broadcasting, insurance, or banking), it pays to take a close look at the parent. The spinoff may be a prelude to a takeover of the parent company. Of course, the spinoff may merely be an attempt to free the parent from the constraints that go along with owning an entity in a regulated industry. However, takeovers of companies that own regulated subsidiaries are very involved and time consuming. One (unspoken) reason for spinning off a regulated subsidiary may be to make the parent company more easily salable. In other instances, the creation of a more attractive takeover target may just be the unintended consequence of such a spinoff.

In Home Shopping's case, there may have been some connection between the decision to pursue the spinoff route and merger discussions. In March 1992, just days after merger talks broke off with its rival in the home-shopping business, QVC Network, Home Shopping announced the spinoff of another division, a money-losing maker of call-processing systems, Precision Systems. The Silver King spinoff announcement followed several weeks later. At the time merger talks were called off, some analysts speculated (in *The Wall Street Journal*) that QVC did not want to buy these extraneous operations. While there were good business reasons for both spinoffs outside of making HSN a more attractive takeover target, the spinoffs certainly had the effect of making HSN a simpler and more appealing acquistion candidate.

Okay, the outcome. In December 1992, even before the spinoff transaction was consummated, Liberty Media (itself a spinoff from Tele-Communications, the country's largest cable provider), signed an agreement to purchase voting control of Home Shopping Network from its founder and largest shareholder, Roy Speer. Days earlier, Liberty had also acted to take control of QVC. The Silver King spinoff was scheduled to proceed as originally planned, though Liberty had now reached agreement to purchase Speer's shares of Silver King, subject to Federal Communications Commission (FCC) approval. Due to regulations restricting ownership by cable operators of broadcast stations, the ultimate control of Silver King was left uncertain. In fact, on the eve of the spinoff, Silver King announced it was unlikely that Liberty Media would ultimately be allowed to purchase the Silver King stake.

It was in this fast-changing (and confused) environment

that the Silver King spinoff took place in January 1993. The stock traded at approximately $5 per share in the first four months after spinoff. This appeared to be an enticing bargain. Although highly leveraged (sometimes an advantage for us), a price of $5 per share meant that Silver King was still trading at less than five times cash flow after interest and taxes. It was unclear, however, what the future of Silver King would look like.

In the past, Silver King's television stations had received a percentage of sales from Home Shopping Network in exchange for airing its shows. What would happen if the Home Shopping Network no longer required Silver King's stations to air its shows? Liberty Media, the new controlling shareholder of HSN, had excellent connections in the cable industry. Maybe HSN could be aired on cable stations directly without using Silver King's stations. Then, Silver King would be left with nothing but a network of major-market television stations reaching 27.5 million homes. Hey, that didn't sound too bad, either.

What happened? After a few months of trading in the $5 area, Silver King moved up to trading in the $10-to-$20 range over the next year. This was due partly to the lifting of the usual post-spinoff selling pressure and partly to speculation (reported in The Wall Street Journal) that Silver King was considering joining with others to form a fifth television network. Several years later, Barry Diller, the well-known media mogul, took control of Silver King to use it as a platform for his new media empire. Certainly, I didn't buy Silver King anticipating this particular series of events. However, buying an ignored property at a low price allowed a lot of room for good things to happen and for value to be ultimately recognized.

Oh, yes. Home Shopping also had some interesting price movement after the spinoff. Its stock actually went up the day the Silver King spinoff was distributed to HSN shareholders. Usually, when a spinoff worth fifty cents per share (one tenth of a share of Silver King selling at $5 per share) is made to the parent company's shareholders, the parent company's shares should fall about fifty cents on the day of the distribution. Instead, Home Shopping's stock went up twenty-five cents per share. If you owned Home Shopping Network stock on the day prior to the distribution, the very next day you were actually paid for the privilege of taking Silver King shares off its hands. The combined value of Home Shopping Network stock and the spun-off Silver King shares created a one-day gain of 12 percent for HSN shareholders. No matter what the academics may say about the efficiency of the stock market, clearly, there are still plenty of inefficiently priced opportunities available — to investors who know where to look, that is.

I almost forgot. Remember Precision Systems? You know, the money-losing maker of call-processing systems that HSN spun off before Silver King? Well, I'm still trying to forget. I never looked at it. After being spun off and trading below $1 per share for several months, within a year the

YOU CAN BE A STOCK MARKET GENIUS

stock traded to $5 and then doubled again over the next two years. You can't win 'em all. (But it would be nice.)

THE TEN COMMANDMENTS

One of the Ten Commandments is "Honor thy father and thy mother." So, logically it follows that paying attention to parents is a good thing. As it happens, this same advice also seems to work well with the parents of spinoffs. Coincidence? I think not.

In the Home Shopping situation, although I was attracted to it partially due to the spinoff, after reading the *Smart Money* article and doing some of my own work I decided to also buy stock in the parent, Home Shopping Network. At a purchase price of $5 before the Silver King spinoff, this worked out to a net purchase price of $4.50 per share after subtracting the initial trading value of Silver King. Looking at the spinoff highlighted the fact that the parent company, Home Shopping Network, was trading at a cheap price. Also, looking at the investment merits of Home Shopping caused me, for comparison purposes, to study its main rival, QVC Network. While I felt Home Shopping was cheap, QVC actually looked even cheaper! Both stocks turned out to be doubles in the next year.

The point here is not to tell you about some more big winners. (Believe me, I've had my share of losers.) The point is that looking at a parent company that is about to be stripped clean of a complicated division can lead to some pretty interesting opportunities. Having said that, let's *charge* ahead.

CASE STUDY

AMERICAN EXPRESS/
LEHMAN BROTHERS

In January 1994, in a widely heralded move, American Express announced its intention to spin off its Lehman Brothers subsidiary as an independent company. The Lehman Brothers spinoff was actually the vestiges of an old-line Wall Street investment-banking partnership that American Express had purchased in the early 1980s. At the time of the purchase, under the leadership of a previous CEO, the idea was to turn American Express into a "financial supermarket." Since after a decade of trying no one could figure out what this meant, the board of American Express had decided to spin off the remains of Lehman to shareholders. When the appropriate filings were made in April 1994, I decided to take a closer look at the "new" Lehman Brothers.

According to the filings and extensive newspaper accounts, Lehman Brothers had the highest expenses per dollar of revenue in the investment industry, had lost money in the last year, and had an extremely volatile earnings history. In addition, insiders, while highly paid as far as salaries and bonuses were concerned, held relatively few shares of stock in the new spinoff. In most companies, and especially on Wall Street, employees act to maximize their compensation. The senior executives of Lehman did not have most of their net worth tied to the fortunes of Lehman's stock. My translation: There was a good chance that when it came time to split up profits between employees and shareholders, shareholders would lose. (You know the drill: two for me—one for you, one for you—two for me, etc.) Unless or until Lehman traded at a big discount to book value and to other investment firms, I wasn't going to be that interested.

But something else caught my eye. According to newspaper accounts, one problem with American Express had been that large institutional investors had no idea what its earnings were going to be for any given period. The main culprit was Lehman's volatile earnings track record. The only thing Wall Street hates more than bad news is *uncertainty*. Overcoming the problem of unpredictable earnings was precisely the goal of the Lehman spinoff. This was also the reasoning behind American Express's earlier sale of its Shearson subsidiary. After the spinoff, American Express would be down to two main businesses, both of which appeared to be less volatile than Lehman.

The first business, categorized by American Express as "Travel Related Services," included the well-known charge card and the world's largest travel agency, as well as the traveler's-check business. Under the new CEO, the plan was to concentrate on and develop these core franchises. Although competition from Visa and MasterCard had eroded some of American Express's business over the last several years, it appeared that much of the problem was due to management inattention. There was clearly going to be a new focus on the basic businesses. As American Express's main product was a charge card requiring full payment every month, its revenues were largely based on fees paid by cardholders and merchants. This seemed more attractive than the credit-card business, which required undertaking greater credit risk. In short, American Express appeared to have a niche in the higher end of the market, with a franchise and brand name that was very hard, if not impossible, to duplicate.

The second business, Investors Diversified Services (IDS), had been growing its earnings at a 20-percent rate for almost ten years. This business consisted of a nationwide group of financial planners who provided clients with overall investment and insurance plans based on the clients' individual needs. The planners often recommended and sold many of the company's own product offerings, such as annuities and mutual funds. Since the financial-planning business is a largely unregulated business dominated by single or small-group practitioners, IDS (now American Express Advisors) was able to provide the comfort, resources, and depth of financial products not easily found in other organizations. This ability to provide services all in one package had allowed IDS to grow its assets under management at a very fast rate. Its revenues were largely derived from the annual fees generated from the investment and insurance products sold to its customers. The bottom line was: IDS also seemed like a valuable and fast-growing niche business.

The exciting thing was that for several months before the spinoff of Lehman Brothers in May 1994, you could buy American Express at a price of $29 per share or less. This price included the value of the Lehman spinoff, estimated in the newspapers to be worth $3 to $5 per American Express share. This meant that the "new," post-spinoff American Express was actually being created for a price between $24 and $26 per share. Since published estimates were that American Express would earn approximately $2.65 per share for 1994 without Lehman Brothers, this worked out to a purchase price of less than ten times earnings.

A look (in *Value Line*) at some large credit-card companies showed their average P/E to be in the low teens. Although I wasn't sure this was the perfect comparison, it appeared that American Express could be priced, on a relative basis, as much as 30 to 40 percent too low. Even though the main charge-card business, under previous management, had suffered some reversals, a new focus on American Express's irreplaceable brand name and high-end market niche gave me some comfort. Also, as previously mentioned, the fee-based nature of American Express's charge card and related businesses seemed more attractive than the greater credit risks being undertaken by the credit-card companies I was using for comparison.

Certainly, IDS, which accounted for approximately 30

percent of American Express's income, looked like a business worth much more than only ten times earnings. After growing at 20 percent per year for such a long time and having a steady income stream from the assets under management, buying this business at a huge discount to the market multiple (of between fourteen and fifteen) seemed like a steal. Although American Express also owned an international bank (most probably worth just ten times earnings), this accounted for less than 10 percent of its total profits.

The bottom line was: At less than ten times earnings, American Express looked very cheap. Once Lehman's confusing and volatile earnings were removed from the picture, I thought that this would become evident to other investors. The only question was, since I wasn't that interested in Lehman, should I buy stock in American Express before or after the spinoff was completed?

As a general rule, even if institutional investors are attracted to a parent company because an undesirable business is being spun off, they will wait until after the spinoff is completed before buying stock in the parent. This practice relieves the institution from having to sell the stock of the unwanted spinoff and removes the risk of the spinoff transaction not being completed. Often institutional buying of the parent's stock immediately after a spinoff has a tendency to drive the price up. That's why, if the parent company appears to be an attractive investment, it is usually worthwhile to buy stock in the parent before the spinoff takes place. Although it is a little more trouble to "create" the bargain purchase by buying stock in the parent before the spinoff is completed, it is usually worth the extra effort—even if you don't get a great price when selling the spinoff shares.

In Lehman's case, since I was happy to "create" American Express at a price between $24 and $26, it was an easy decision to buy it at $29 before the spinoff. The Lehman stock, which I ended up keeping (I hate selling spinoffs), started trading at about $18.50 per share. (As one share of Lehman was distributed for every five shares of American Express owned, this worked out to a value of about $3.75 per American Express share.) American Express stock did rise 1⅛ the first day of trading after the Lehman distribution, so buying before the spinoff was a good move. It was also a good move for the long term. American Express proceeded to reach $36 per share in the first year after the spinoff, for a gain of over 40 percent in one year.

By the way, a little over six months after the spinoff, Warren Buffett announced that he had purchased just under 10 percent of American Express. Apparently, the spinoff and sale of unrelated businesses had unmasked American Express to be a "Warren Buffett" company—a compelling bargain with a strong brand name and an attractive market niche.

See—paying attention to parents—who'd 'a' thunk it?

PARTIAL SPINOFFS

I never like to work too hard to understand an investment. So if a potential investment is too complicated or difficult to understand, I'd rather skip it and find something easier to figure out. That's why this next area, partial spin-offs, is so attractive to me. Here is an area where boning up on first-grade math skills (especially subtraction) is the key to success.

In a partial spinoff transaction, a company decides to spin off or sell only a portion of one of its divisions. Instead of spinning off 100-percent ownership in a division to its share-holders, only a portion of the division's stock is distributed to parent-company shareholders or sold to the general pub-lic; the parent company retains the remainder of the divi-sion's stock. For example, if XYZ Corporation distributes a 20-percent interest in its Widget division to its shareholders, 20 percent of Widget's outstanding shares will trade pub-licly while 80 percent will still be owned by XYZ.

Companies may pursue a partial-spinoff strategy for sev-eral reasons. Sometimes a corporation may need to raise capital. Selling off a portion of a division while still retain-ing management control may be an attractive option. At other times the motivation for pursuing a partial spinoff is to highlight a particular division's true value to the market-place. Its value may be masked when buried among the par-ent company's other businesses. A separate stock price for that division enables investors to value the division indepen-dently. It also allows for incentive compensation for the division's managers to be based directly on divisional perfor-mance.

The benefits of investigating partial spinoffs are twofold.

First, in the case where shares in the partial spinoff are distributed directly to parent-company shareholders, spinoff shares should perform well for most of the same reasons that 100-percent spinoffs do. In the case where a partial stake in a division is *sold directly* to the public (through an Initial Public Offering, known as an IPO), your opportunity is probably not as good. This is because the people who buy stock in the public offering are not being handed stock they don't want. A stock price depressed by indiscriminate selling is therefore not likely.

Your second opportunity comes from something else. Here's where you break out your first-grade math skills. Once the stock of the partial spinoff is publicly trading, the market has effectively valued the spun-off division. If the Widget division of XYZ Corporation has 10 million shares outstanding and 2 million are sold to the public for $20 per share, that means XYZ still owns 8 million shares of Widget. The value of those shares works out to $160 million (8 million shares multiplied by a $20 share price—okay, second-grade math).

Now comes your second opportunity. By doing this simple math, you now know two things. Of course, you know the value of XYZ's 80-percent stake in Widget—$160 million. However, you also know the value the market places on all the rest of XYZ's businesses: that value is equal to the market value of XYZ less $160 million. Here's how it works: If XYZ has a market value of $500 million, and its 80-percent Widget stake is valued by the market at $160 million, that implies a net value of $340 million for the rest of XYZ's businesses.

Where will that little piece of trivia get you? Let's see.

CASE STUDY

THE CHEAPER SIDE OF SEARS

In September 1992, Sears announced its intention to sell a 20-percent stake in two of its subsidiaries to the public. Sears's management had been under pressure to improve the performance of its stock price for years. It was Sears's contention that the value of the two subsidiaries, Dean Witter (including Discover) and Allstate Insurance, was not adequately reflected in Sears's stock price. In the case of Dean Witter, Sears also announced its intention to distribute its remaining 80-percent interest directly to shareholders at a later date, some time in 1993.

Why was this interesting? After all, before the announcement, Sears was a conglomerate that owned Dean Witter, Allstate, and the well-known department store chain. It was no secret that Sears had owned all of these businesses for years. Sears was widely followed by Wall Street analysts. So why, all of a sudden, was this an investment opportunity? Sears was merely selling or distributing businesses it already owned.

The answer is that not only was Sears going to be high-lighting the market value of Dean Witter and Allstate — through the public trading of these two divisions — it was also going to be revealing something else. By taking Sears's stock price and subtracting the market value of its remaining stakes in Dean Witter and Allstate, a value for the rest of Sears's assets, primarily the department store, could be calculated. Big deal? A very big deal. Let's see why.

A 20-percent stake in Dean Witter was sold by Sears in February 1993. Sears's stated intention was to spin off (by a distribution directly to Sears shareholders) its remaining 80-percent interest in Dean Witter in the next several months. In the beginning of June, Sears sold a 20-percent stake in Allstate for $27 a share. By the beginning of July, just before Sears's distribution of its remaining stake in Dean Witter, this is how things stood: Dean Witter's stock was trading at approximately $37 per share; Allstate's stock was trading around $29; Sears's stock stood at about $54.

The math worked like this. Sears had announced that it would distribute its remaining 80-percent stake in Dean Witter. According to the announcement, this meant that, for every 100 shares of Sears, a distribution of 40 shares of Dean Witter would be made. (Sears was distributing 136 million shares of Dean Witter and had approximately 340 million shares outstanding—so the distribution ratio was 136/340 or .4.) Therefore, in mid-July, each Sears share-holder would receive shares in Dean Witter worth approximately .4 (the announced distribution ratio) multiplied by $37 (the trading price of Dean Witter's stock), or approximately $15 worth of Dean Witter stock for each share of Sears owned.

Since Sears was trading at $54 per share before the distribution, this translated to a net price of $39 for the remainder of Sears. What was that remainder? Primarily, it was Sears's remaining 80-percent stake in Allstate, its foreign and domestic department-store business, and various real-estate businesses (including Coldwell Banker). However, we also knew something else: the market value of Sears's 80-percent stake in Allstate.

Sears owned approximately 340 million shares of Allstate. Sears, itself, also happened to have approximately 340 million shares outstanding. This meant that if you owned a share of Sears you also indirectly owned a share of Allstate. With Allstate at about $29, for about $10 per share ($39 net stock price less $29 price of Allstate), you were getting the foreign and domestic Sears department-store business and its real-estate business. Was this a bargain?

Michael Price, a well-known fund manager, sure thought so. In a *Barron's* interview (July 5, 1993), he laid out the case straightforwardly:

> That $54 a share includes one share of Allstate, which is at $28. So that leaves $26. Then you get 0.4 share of Dean Witter, which is $15. That leaves $10 or $11. About

$2 or $3 of that is Sears Mexico and Sears Canada. That leaves about $8. Coldwell Banker is worth $2 or $3 a share. So that leaves $5 a share, or a market cap of about $1.5 billion for the retailer—with $27 billion in sales. The new management seems very focused. It's an almost debt-free retailer with huge real-estate opportunities.

I told you, I never like to work too hard to understand an investment. A quick check revealed that indeed Price was right. Sears was cheap. With $27 billion in sales and 340 million shares outstanding, Sears had $79 per share in sales. If those sales could be purchased for $5 a share (pretty much debt free), then that worked out to a purchase price of just over 6 percent of sales (5 divided by 79). On the other hand, a look at J. C. Penney showed sales of about $78 per share and a market price of about $44 per share—that was over 56 percent of sales. Of course, there are many other measures of relative value (earnings, for instance), but all indications were that the domestic retail business of Sears could be created at an incredibly cheap price.

By the way, although I am a strong advocate of doing your own work, this doesn't mean I'm against "stealing" other people's ideas. It's a big world out there. You can't begin to cover everything yourself. That's why, if you read about an investment situation that falls into one of the categories covered in this book, it's often productive to take a closer look. If either the logic of the situation is compelling or the advice comes from a short list of reliable experts (to be named later), "stealing" can be a profitable practice.

Of course, "stealing" refers to stealing an idea (technically, without the use of deadly force). Unfortunately, you still have to do your own homework. In the Sears case, in addition to the *Barron's* article, Michael Price gave a similar interview to *Fortune* magazine in mid-June. So even if you hadn't followed the Sears spinoff story for the many months it appeared in the business press—or you followed the story but neglected to do the math yourself—there were at least two widely available opportunities to pirate a good idea. If you know the types of situation you're looking for, such as partial spinoffs, these type of opportunities are much easier to spot.

Buying Sears stock also worked out quite well. (We'll get to some losers . . . later.) After the Dean Witter distribution, the $39 remaining investment in Sears was up 50 percent over the next several months. Allstate was only up from $29 to $33 during this period. Obviously, the market finally took notice of the inherent value of Sears's other assets.

(For the advanced students: Yes, it was possible to simultaneously buy Sears stock and short Allstate stock, creating only the portion of Sears that was clearly a bargain. In some cases, this is a smart way to play, especially when the value of the cheap portion—a $5-per-share department-store purchase—is a small part of the purchase price: $39, post Dean Witter distribution. However, in this case, the disparity between the bargain purchase price of the department-store segment and true value was so huge, no such fancy tactics were necessary.)

INSIDER TIPS: A DO-IT-YOURSELF GUIDE

Insiders. I may have already mentioned that looking to see what insiders are doing is a good way to find attractive spinoff opportunities. (Okay, so maybe I've beaten you over the head with it.) The thinking is that if insiders own a large amount of stock or options, their interests and the interests of shareholders will be closely aligned. But, did you know there are times when insiders may benefit when a spinoff trades at a low price? Did you know there are some situations where insiders come out ahead when you *don't* buy stock in a new spinoff? Did you know you could gain a large advantage by spotting these situations? Well, it's all true.

Spinoffs are a unique animal. In the usual case, when a company first sells stock publicly an elaborate negotiation takes place. The underwriter (the investment firm that takes a company public) and the owners of the company engage in a discussion about the price at which the company's stock should be sold in its initial offering. Although the price is set based on market factors, in most cases there is a good deal of subjectivity involved. The company's owners want the stock to be sold at a high price so that the most money will be raised. The underwriter will usually prefer a lower price, so that investors who buy stock in the offering can make some money. (That way, the next new issue they underwrite will be easier to sell.) In any event, an arms-length negotiation takes place and a price is set. In a spinoff situation no such discussion takes place.

Instead, shares of a spinoff are distributed directly to parent-company shareholders and the spinoff's price is left to market forces. Often, management's incentive-stock-option plan is based on this initial trading price. The lower the price of the spinoff, the lower the exercise price of the incentive option. (E.g., if a spinoff initially trades at $5 per share, management receives the right to buy shares at $5; an $8 initial price would require management to pay $8 for their stock.) In these situations, it is to management's benefit to promote interest in the spinoff's stock *after* this price is set by the market, not before.

In other words, don't expect bullish pronouncements or presentations about a new spinoff until a price has been established for management's incentive stock options. This price can be set after a day of trading, a week, a month, or more. Sometimes, a management's silence about the merits of a new spinoff may not be bad news; in some cases, this silence may actually be golden. If you are attracted to a particular spinoff situation, it may pay to check out the SEC filings for information about when the pricing of management's stock options is to be set. In a situation where management's option package is substantial, it may be a good idea to establish a portion of your stock position before management becomes incentivized to start promoting the new spinoff's stock. Eventually, management and shareholders will be playing on the same team, but it's often helpful to know when the "game" begins.

There are very few investment areas where insiders have such one-sided control in creating a new publicly-traded company. Because of this unique quality, analyzing the actions and motives of insiders in spinoff situations is of particular benefit. Since all shareholders of a parent company either receive shares in a new spinoff or have the equal right to buy shares in a new spinoff, there are few fairness issues that come up when dividing assets and liabilities between parent and spinoff. There are, however, ways that insiders can use their relatively unchecked ability to set the structure and terms of a spinoff to gain an advantage for themselves. Of course, by focusing on the motives of management and other insiders you can turn this advantage for insiders into an advantage for yourself. This is particularly true when it comes to analyzing this next method of establishing a new spinoff company.

BUY ALL RIGHTS

Occasionally, instead of merely distributing the shares in a spinoff to shareholders free of charge, a parent company may give its shareholders the right to *buy* stock in one of its subsidiaries or divisions. One way to accomplish this is through something called a *rights offering*. Most rights offerings, at least the type that most investors are familiar with, do not involve spinoffs. However, on the rare occasions that a rights offering is used to effect a spinoff, it is worthwhile to pay extra close attention. Why? Come on—you should know this one by now. (Oh, all right—psst—because you can make a lot of money!)

A rights offering is most commonly used when a company seeks to raise additional capital. In the usual case, rights are distributed to a company's current shareholders. These rights, together with cash or securities, allow shareholders to purchase additional shares (usually at a discount to the current market price). By giving all shareholders the right (but not the obligation) to buy stock at a discounted price, a company can raise needed capital while giving all shareholders an equal chance to buy the newly issued stock. If current shareholders choose to participate in the rights offering by exercising their right to buy additional stock, their interests are not diluted by the company's sale of new stock at a low price. Alternatively, if shareholders do not wish to purchase additional stock, they can often sell the rights they've received to participate in the bargain purchase on the open market. Rights that are not exercised or sold expire worthless after a set time period.

Rights offerings are also unhappily familiar to owners of closed-end funds. Closed-end funds, whether equity or bond funds, are like mutual funds except that the amount of fund shares issued is fixed (e.g., 20 million shares are sold at $10 per share in a public offering and those 20 million shares are bought and sold just like a common stock). One way for a closed-end fund to raise additional capital (and thereby raise the fund manager's advisory fees) is to issue more shares through a rights offering. As a general rule, only the fund manager of the closed-end fund benefits from this type of rights offering.

But now for the good news. When it comes to the spinoff area, rights offerings can be an extraordinary opportunity for enterprising investors like you. Rights offerings are obscure and often confusing. Throw in the neglect and disinterest displayed by most institutional investors towards spinoffs, and you have an explosive combination. Generally, a parent company will distribute to its shareholders rights (free of charge) to buy shares in a spinoff. Holders of the rights will then have the right to buy shares in the spinoff for the next thirty or sixty days at a fixed dollar price or for a specified amount of other securities. The rights are usually transferable, which means that shareholders who do not wish to purchase shares of the spinoff can sell their rights in the open market and investors who are not shareholders of the parent can participate in the rights offering by buying rights in the marketplace.

The timing, terms, and details of each rights offering are different. The important thing to remember is this: Any time you read about a spinoff being accomplished through a rights offering, stop whatever you're doing and take a look. (Don't worry, they're quite rare.) Just looking will already put you in an elite (though strange) group, but—more important—you will be concentrating your efforts in an area even more potentially lucrative than ordinary spinoffs. You won't have to waste too much effort either. Before you get knee deep into the intricacies of a particular situation, a quick examination of some superficial aspects of the rights offering and the motives of insiders will either get you excited enough to do some more work or persuade you to spend your time elsewhere.

So why does combining a spinoff with a rights offering create such a profitable opportunity? After all, the bargain element of a standard spinoff—indiscriminate selling of the unwanted spinoff stock by parent-company shareholders—is not present in a rights offering. In fact, in a rights offering almost the opposite takes place. Shareholders who use their rights to purchase shares are actually making an affirmative choice to *buy* stock in the new spinoff. Even the bargain element of a standard rights offering is not present in this situation. Unlike the usual rights offering, the rights do not ensure a bargain purchase. This is because, at the time of the offering, it is not known whether the spinoff will trade above or below the purchase price set in the rights offering. So where does the profit opportunity come from?

The answer lies in the very nature of a rights offering. If stock in a new spinoff is sold by the parent company through a rights offering, the parent company has, by definition, chosen not to pursue other alternatives. These alternatives could have included selling the spinoff's businesses to another company or selling the spinoff to the public at large through an underwritten public offering—both of which require the directors of the parent company, as fiduciaries, to seek the highest price possible for selling the spinoff's assets. But if the parent company uses a rights offering to sell the spinoff company to its own shareholders there is no need to seek the highest possible price. In fact, limiting initial buyers of the spinoff to parent-company shareholders and to investors who purchase rights in the open market is not usually the best way to maximize proceeds from the sale of the spinoff's businesses. However, in a rights offering, since all shareholders of the parent have an equal opportunity to purchase stock in the spinoff—even if a bargain sale is made—shareholders have been treated equally and fairly.

While there is a general tendency for a spinoff to be offered at an attractive price in a rights offering (*note:* investors who buy rights in the open market must add the purchase price of the rights to the offering price to figure out their total cost), examining the structure of a rights offering can give important additional clues. One telltale sign of a bargain offering price is the inclusion of *oversubscription* privileges in a rights offering. Oversubscription privileges give investors who purchase spinoff stock in the rights offering the right to buy additional spinoff shares if the rights offering is not fully subscribed. Since rights are obscure, require the payment of additional consideration, and usually trade illiquidly for small sums of money (relative to the value of parent-company holdings), there are often times when rights holders neither exercise nor sell their rights. In a case where rights to buy 3,000,000 shares are distributed, but rights to buy 1,000,000 shares expire unused, oversubscription privileges allow those rights holders who purchase stock in the offering an additional opportunity to purchase the remaining 1,000,000 shares on a pro-rata basis.

Insiders who wish to increase their percentage ownership in a new spinoff at a bargain price can do so by including oversubscription privileges in the rights offering. In certain cases, insiders may be required to disclose their intention to oversubscribe for shares in the new spinoff in the SEC filings. The implications of this type of disclosure are obvious. Keep one more point in mind: When oversubscription privileges are involved, the less publicized the rights offering (and the lower the trading price of the rights), the less likely it is for rights holders to purchase stock in the rights offering, and the better the opportunity for insiders and enterprising investors to pick up spinoff shares at a bargain price.

While we could review other ways the rights-offering process can result in big spinoff profits, it is more important to remember one simple concept: no matter how a transaction is structured, if you can figure out what's in it for the insiders, you will have discovered one of the most important keys to selecting the best spinoff opportunities. In this next example—one of the most complicated and lucrative spinoff transactions of all time—practically the only way to figure out what was going on was to keep a close eye on the insiders.

In fact, the spinoff was structured in such a complex and uninviting fashion that I wondered whether the insiders had actually planned it that way. While I usually try to avoid investment situations that are difficult to understand, in this case there was a good reason to make an exception. After I determined that insiders had every reason to hope I wouldn't buy stock in the new spinoff, I had every reason to put in the time and effort required to understand what was happening.

While this situation may be too complex for most investors, that's not the important point. Even the experts blew this one. The only point you really need to take away is this: Don't forget to check out the motives of insiders. That point should come through loud and clear.

So let's see how to make some real money.

CASE STUDY ✏ ✏ ✏
LIBERTY MEDIA/
TELE-COMMUNICATIONS

Question: How do you make a half billion dollars in less than two years?

Answer: Start with $50 million and ask John Malone. He did it.

John Malone, CEO of Tele-Communications, took advantage of the spinoff process to create a situation that proved to be one of the great spinoff opportunities of all time. Anyone who participated in the Liberty Media rights offering, a spinoff from Tele-Communications, was able to earn ten times his initial investment in less than two years. Although all shareholders of Tele-Communications (TCI), the parent company, had an equal opportunity to participate in the rights offering (and the whole world had the ability to purchase these same rights), the offering was artfully designed to create the most upside potential for those who participated, while simultaneously discouraging most investors from taking advantage of the opportunity.

The entire spinoff was followed closely by *The Wall Street Journal* (much of it on the front page), yet almost everyone in the investment community missed this chance to make a quick fortune. Hopefully, the next time an opportunity like this rolls around, everyone will pass right by it again—everyone, that is, except for you.

The whole scenario began in January 1990. Tele-Communications, the country's largest cable operator, announced its preliminary intention to spin off its programming assets (like QVC and the Family Channel) and some of its minority interests in cable-television systems—assets estimated to be worth nearly $3 billion. The announcement was made in response to continuing pressure from Washington to lessen the influence of large cable operators, and Tele-Communications in particular, on the cable industry. Under the leadership of John Malone, Tele-Communications had become a behemoth in the industry, wielding its considerable power to, among other things, dictate which program providers would be carried on its cable systems and

on what terms. Due to its size (almost 25 percent of all cable households), TCI was often in a position to make or
break the launch of a new cable channel and in some cases
to use its clout to purchase equity interests in new channels.
In response to what was perceived to be Malone's tight control over the industry, one proposal much discussed in
Washington was legislation to limit the ability of cable-
system operators to own interests in program providers.

The stated hope of the spinoff was to alleviate some of the
pressure from Washington, and to give Tele-Communications greater flexibility, by separating the company's programming assets from its controlled cable systems. The
other announced reason for the spinoff was more typical—
shareholder value. The hope was that the spinoff would
highlight the value of the parent company's ownership
stakes in programming assets and its minority stakes in other
cable systems. It was thought that these stakes had been lost
amid TCI's large portfolio of cable properties.

In March of 1990, *The Wall Street Journal* reported a new
development. Rather than proceed with a usual spinoff,
Tele-Communications had chosen to use a rights offering to
effect the spinoff of its programming and other cable properties. Shareholders were to receive rights that would entitle
them to exchange some of their TCI stock for shares in the
new company. The rights offering was selected primarily for
tax reasons. (If a rights offering is structured correctly, shareholders are only taxed based on the value of the rights received.)

The March announcement also disclosed something else. The spinoff would not be nearly as large as initially suggested. TCI was no longer planning to spin off its $1 billion stake in Turner Broadcasting. In October 1990, just before the preliminary SEC filings were made, the distribution of Tele-Communications's 50-percent stake in the Discovery Channel was also taken off the table. The value of the entity to be spun off had shrunk to well under 50 percent of original expectations. In fact, SEC filings made in November of 1990 and revised in January 1991 disclosed that the estimated value of the assets to be spun off into the new entity, Liberty Media, were down to approximately $600 million. As TCI had a total market capitalization of approximately $15 billion (about $6 billion of equity value and $9 billion in debt), the size of the Liberty spinoff was going to represent a drop in the bucket relative to the whole of Tele-Communications. In other words, Liberty was going to be an unimportant sideshow as far as most institutional investors were concerned (and potentially a classic spinoff opportunity for us).

According to newspaper accounts in January 1991, Liberty's portfolio of assets was going to include minority interests in fourteen cable franchises serving 1.6 million subscribers, and interests in twenty-six other entities including eleven regional sports networks, as well as minority interests in The Family Channel, American Movie Classics, Black Entertainment Television, and the QVC Shopping Network. These assets were estimated by Tele-Communications to have a value of approximately $600 million, more or less equally divided between cable and programming interests. *The Wall Street Journal* reported that "Liberty will be a much smaller company than some had expected, issuing only about two million shares. On a fully diluted basis, Tele-Communications has about 415 million shares outstanding." According to the *Journal*, analysts described the almost-400-page prospectus as "one of the most complex transactions of its kind" and a cause of confusion to investors. Due to the exclusion of TCI's interests in Turner Broadcasting and the Discovery Channel, some analysts felt that "Liberty may be perceived as a less attractive investment." The *Journal* went on to report, "On a pro forma basis, for the nine months ended Sept. 30, 1990, Liberty reported a loss of $20.4 million after a preferred stock dividend requirement, and a $9.77 a share loss."

In sum, the picture of Liberty painted for most investors did not exactly shout, "Come on in, the water's fine!" If this basic description wasn't discouraging enough, there was still plenty more to come. Tele-Communications's shareholders were to receive one transferable right for every 200 shares they owned. Each right, together with sixteen shares of Tele-Communications, could then be exchanged for one share of Liberty Media. (The rights expired after thirty days.) At a price of $16 for a share of TCI, this translated to a purchase price of $256 per share of Liberty (sixteen shares of TCI at $16 each). As stated, there were approximately 415 million fully diluted shares of TCI, a distribution of one right (to buy one share of Liberty) for every 200 TCI shares held translated into the approximately 2.1 million shares of Liberty to be issued.

For an institution that owned stock in a corporation with over 400 million shares, a stock with a capitalization of only 2 million shares would generally be considered not only risky and inappropriate, but entirely too illiquid to be included in its portfolio. A price of over $250 per share is also considered very awkward. Very few institutions would be willing to trade a very liquid stock with over 400 million shares outstanding for a small amount of a very illiquid stock. A search through the SEC filings for an explanation for the desire to have only 2 million shares of Liberty outstanding priced at $256 per share—as opposed to a more usual 20 million shares priced at approximately $26, or 40 million shares priced around $13—revealed the following clarification: "The exchange rates at which shares of [Liberty stock] will be issued in exchange for [TCI stock] were selected solely for the purpose of limiting the aggregate number of shares of [Liberty] common stock initially to be issued to a maximum of approximately 2,000,000 shares. The exchange rates are not intended to be any indicator of the value of [Liberty's] securities." My translation: "We picked 2,000,000 shares because we wanted Liberty stock to appear unattractive to TCI shareholders."

Why do I say this? What advantage was there for Liberty to appear unattractive? For starters, the rights offering was structured so that the amount of Liberty shares issued would be equal to the amount of rights exercised. In other words, if only 1 million rights were exercised to purchase Liberty stock, only 1 million shares of Liberty would be issued—not the theoretical maximum of 2 million shares, if all TCI holders exercised their right to purchase stock. A sale of 1 million shares in exchange for $256 worth of TCI stock would equal a purchase price of $256 million for all of the common equity in Liberty Media (instead of a potential $512 million cost if all 2 million shares were purchased). Since Liberty would still own the same assets, regardless of whether 1 million shares of common stock were issued or 2 million shares, anyone primarily interested in Liberty's upside potential would much prefer to split that potential among fewer shares.

The deal had still another twist. Any common stock (the stock entitled to all upside appreciation in the value of Liberty) not sold in the rights offering would be replaced by preferred stock to be owned by Tele-Communications. Since, as stated, TCI was transferring the same assets to Liberty regardless of whether $250 million worth of Liberty stock was sold or $500 million, this $250 million shortfall was to be made up through the issuance of $250 million of Liberty preferred stock to TCI. The terms of the preferred stock to be issued were very advantageous to Liberty. The bottom line was: The fewer shareholders that participated in the Liberty offering, the more leveraged the upside potential for Liberty's stock. Better still, this leveraged upside would be achieved not through the issuance of debt but through the issuance of low-cost preferred stock. Since this preferred stock required no cash payments for fifteen years, carried a low rate of 6 percent, and had a fixed redemption price (i.e., no upside potential), this was clearly an attractive way to achieve the benefits of leverage for Liberty common stock—without the risks of taking on debt.

What were TCI's insiders doing in the midst of all this confusion? For one thing, they weren't giving away free advice. According to *The Wall Street Journal*, "Tele-Communications' top two executives, Chairman Bob Magness and President John Malone, have advised the company they each currently intend to exercise at least 50 percent of their exchange rights." Certainly not a rousing endorsement. But if you looked a bit closer there were some helpful hints available.

In the prospectus issued for the rights offering, located under the heading "Executive Compensation," the following statement was found: "Pursuant to Dr. Malone's employment agreement, in lieu of cash compensation for his services to [Liberty], Dr. Malone will be granted nontransferable options to purchase 100,000 shares of [Liberty stock] at a price per share equal to $256." This translated to an option, not including any shares of Liberty purchased by Malone in the rights offering, for over $25 million worth of Liberty stock. Since, according to the same SEC filing, Malone owned approximately $50 million worth of TCI stock, the success of Liberty was going to be of material significance even to John Malone. If 2 million shares of Liberty were issued, an option on 100,000 shares was equal to an option on 5 percent of the total company. At 1 million shares of Liberty outstanding, this translated to a 10-percent share of Liberty's upside.

Looking a bit further, Liberty wasn't nearly as bad off as the newspaper summaries made it appear. The pro forma loss of $9.77 per share for the most recent nine-month period wasn't the whole story. The earnings (or lack of earnings) shown in the pro forma statements included the operations of only a very small portion of Liberty's assets. Since the bulk of Liberty's assets were made up of equity stakes in other companies, the revenues and earnings of most of these interests were not consolidated into Liberty's income statement. (These stakes merely appeared on Liberty's balance sheet at cost.) Even *Forbes* magazine (which I enjoy reading) completely blew it. Citing Liberty's low level of revenues and earnings (I guess they didn't read the SEC filing), *Forbes* stated, "If you're a TCI shareholder, pass on the swap [exchanging TCI shares for Liberty shares through the rights offering]. If you're considering buying Liberty [stock] . . . , don't chase it." So, while it's great to read business publications to find new ideas, it still pays to remember Rule #1: Do your own work. (I'm sorry, but this work does include at least *reading* the pro forma financial statements.)

There was something else about Liberty that looked very exciting. According to the prospectus, management of TCI had the "expectation that [Liberty's] Common Stock will initially represent only an interest in any future growth of [Liberty]". What was this worth? Well, let's see. Tele-Communications held approximately $15 billion of cable assets. Liberty was going to be controlled by the same group of managers as Tele-Communications. Liberty was set up as a vehicle for TCI's programming ventures. If John Malone was going to receive a big chunk of Liberty's upside, maybe TCI could use some of its considerable muscle to help out little Liberty. Certainly, a new cable channel might benefit from cutting Liberty in for a piece of its equity. Perhaps this would help the new channel's chances of being carried over Tele-Communications's vast cable network. Maybe Liberty could start up its own cable channels. These new cable channnels would also have a huge head start if made available to all of TCI's subscribers. Hmmm . . . so how many ways would all this upside be split?

The answer was, it depended on how many of Tele-Communications's shareholders decided to use their rights to exchange shares of TCI for shares of Liberty. One press report summed up the general consensus nicely: "Liberty's problems include an illiquid stock, a terribly complicated asset and capital structure, and lack of initial cash flow from its investments." A Bear Stearns analyst added, "We view this offer as having very limited appeal for most fund managers." Shearson Lehman stated, "to give up [TCI] to participate in Liberty, a highly uncertain value with limited liquidity, doesn't strike us an especially good trade at virtually any price for most institutional investors." It should have been no surprise, then, when only about 36 percent of eligible rights to buy Liberty stock were exercised, resulting in only slightly more than 700,000 Liberty shares of a possible 2 million being issued.

The rights to buy shares in Liberty for $256 worth of TCI stock were freely traded and could have been purchased by anyone who so desired for a period of thirty days. The rights were available at a price of less than $1 per right—meaning the owner of 200 shares of TCI ($3,000 of TCI stock) received a right worth less than $1.

Most shareholders of TCI neither exercised nor sold their rights. Of course, Tele-Communications's top two executives, Bob Magness and John Malone, did end up exercising all of their rights to buy shares in Liberty after all. Together with his 100,000 options, Malone had been able to keep nearly 20 percent of Liberty's upside for himself, compared with his participation in less than 2 percent of TCI's upside. Although CEO of both entities, Malone was clearly incentivized to use TCI's considerable clout in the cable industry to make sure that Liberty thrived. Then again, all TCI shareholders had had an equal opportunity to participate in Liberty's future—even if they weren't exactly led by the hand.

According to *Multichannel News*, a publication covering the cable industry,

> TCI officials expected fewer than 50 percent of the eligible shares to participate. But as TCI disclosed details of

the plan, Wall Street soured on Liberty's illiquid stock, complicated asset and capital structure and lack of initial cash flow.

John Malone, chairman of Liberty and president and CEO of TCI said he was indifferent to, not disappointed by, Wall Street's lack of enthusiasm.

Even though Liberty's shareholder meetings can be held "in one telephone booth," Malone said that in structuring the deal, TCI executives realized it wouldn't be for everybody.

"People had to make up their own minds," Malone said. "You can get yourself into trouble convincing people to get into things."

Sure. That makes sense. When you make ten times your initial investment in less than two years (to be fair, an outcome not even Malone could have expected), think of all the horrible tax problems you could cause unsuspecting investors.

P.S. Less than a year after the rights offering, Liberty split its stock—twenty for one—the greater liquidity attracting both institutional investors and analysts.

SPINOFFS: A QUICK SUMMARY

Before we leave the spinoff area, let's take a moment to review some highlights:

1. Spinoffs, in general, beat the market.
2. Picking your spots, within the spinoff universe, can result in even better results than the average spinoff.
3. Certain characteristics point to an exceptional spinoff opportunity:
   a. Institutions don't want the spinoff (and not because of the investment merits).
   b. Insiders want the spinoff.
   c. A previously hidden investment opportunity is uncovered by the spinoff transaction (e.g., a cheap stock, a great business, a leveraged risk/reward situation).
4. You can locate and analyze new spinoff prospects by reading the business press and following up with SEC filings.
5. Paying attention to "parents" can pay off handsomely.
6. Partial spinoffs and rights offerings create unique investment opportunities.
7. Oh, yes. Keep an eye on the insiders. (Did I already mention that?)

And some additional points:

1. Reruns of *Gilligan's Island* are boring.
2. "Stealing" can be a good thing.
3. Don't ask stupid questions at Lutèce.

Hey. Why didn't I just say it like this in the first place?

Chapter 4

DON'T TRY THIS AT HOME

RISK ARBITRAGE AND
MERGER SECURITIES

• • •

"Don't try this at home."

—third-base coach to runner who just stole third

RISK ARBITRAGE

Risk (or merger) arbitrage is the business of buying stock in a company that is subject to an announced merger or takeover. Contrary to popular belief (fostered by the exploits of the most infamous arbitrageur, Ivan Boesky, and numerous other insider trading scandals), risk arbitrage generally involves the purchase of a stock *after* a merger announcement is already made. In its simplest form, Company A announces that it has agreed to acquire all of Company B's stock for $40 per share. Prior to the announcement, Company B traded at $25 per share; after the announcement, Company B's shares trade at $38, not at the proposed acquisition price of $40 per share. A *risk arbitrageur* (fancy term for the guy who buys the stock at $38) attempts to profit from this discrepancy. Far from a riskless transaction, the arbitrageur takes on two risks.

First, the deal may not go through for a variety of reasons. These may include regulatory problems, financing problems, extraordinary changes in a company's business, discoveries during the due-diligence process (if you've ever purchased a home, this is sort of the house inspection of the merger world), personality problems, or any number of legally justifiable reasons people use when they change their mind. In the event of a broken deal, Company B's shares may fall back to the predeal price of $25 or even lower, resulting in big losses for the arbitrageur. The second risk that the arbitrageur is underwriting is the timing risk. Depending upon the type of deal and industry involved, merger deals can take from one to eighteen months to close. Part of the $2 spread made by the arbitrageur is payment for the time value of laying out $38 before the close of the deal (when the acquirer purchases all of company B's shares at $40). One of the arbitrageur's jobs is to assess the time required for the merger to be consummated.

Over the last decade, dozens of investment firms and partnerships have entered the risk arbitrage area, once considered a backwater of the securities business. This has made risk arbitrage a very competitive business despite the large volume of mergers. The ability of these firms to follow developments in deals all day long, armed with the advice of antitrust counsel, securities lawyers, and industry-specific investment experts, makes this a very difficult investment strategy for the individual to try at home. In addition, the degree of competition keeps the spread between the stock price and the acquisition price relatively low, making risk-adjusted profits tougher to come by.

Still want to play? Think I'm just trying to throw cold water on your good time? Like the sound of *risk arbitrageur* (ar-be-trah-zhure)? Thick as a doorpost? Maybe the next few examples will help you see it my way.

CASE STUDY
FLORIDA CYPRESS GARDENS/
HARCOURT BRACE JOVANOVICH

This is one of the first deals I invested in when I started out in business for myself. In April 1985, Harcourt Brace Jovanovich (HBJ), the book publisher and owner of Sea World, announced that an acquisition agreement had been reached with Florida Cypress Gardens. Since I remembered and had fond memories of visiting Cypress Gardens as a child, the idea of buying stock in Florida Cypress Gardens gave me a warm and fuzzy feeling inside, in addition to being an investment in a company I knew and understood well. As theme parks go, Cypress Gardens, with its rare and exotic gardens, beautifully landscaped walks, and spectacular water-ski shows (complete with waterskiing Santa Clauses and chorus girls), was a unique and special place. (All right, leave me alone—I was only seven and I'm trying to tell a story here.)

Under the terms of the merger agreement, each share of Florida Cypress Gardens would be exchanged for .16 of a share of Harcourt Brace. The deal was subject to certain requirements including approval by shareholders of Florida

Cypress Gardens. A shareholder meeting was to be held approximately three months after the signing of the merger agreement. Since the chairman of Cypress Gardens owned 44 percent of the stock outstanding, I didn't think shareholder approval was much of a risk. On the HBJ side, the value of the deal was so small relative to the size of Harcourt Brace that no shareholder vote was even required.

The deal certainly seemed to make sense for shareholders of Florida Cypress Gardens. Before the deal was announced, the stock traded at only $4.50 per share. As Harcourt Brace stock was trading at $51.875, a purchase price for Cypress Gardens of .16 of a share of HBJ translated to a buyout value of $8.30 per share (.16 multiplied by $51.875). After the announcement, shares of Cypress Gardens rose $3 per share to a price of $7.50. This meant that, even after a dramatic 66-percent rise in value ($3 gain on original price of $4.50), there was still a sizable profit left to be made by arbitrageurs. An arbitrageur could purchase stock in Cypress Gardens at $7.50 and, if the deal closed, make eighty cents per share (the spread). After about three months, each share purchased at $7.50 would be exchanged for $8.30 worth of HBJ stock. An eighty-cent profit on an investment of $7.50 equaled a return of 10.67 percent in about three months, or on a compounded basis—nearly 50 percent annualized ($1.1067 \times 1.1067 \times 1.1067 \times 1.1067$—you do the math— compound interest is great, isn't it?).

The only flaw in the equation was that the $8.30 acquisition price was payable in stock, not cash. If HBJ stock declined even 5 or 10 percent during the three months prior to the closing of the deal, the expected eighty-cent profit could be greatly reduced or erased entirely. To eliminate this risk, an arbitrageur would generally sell the shares of HBJ *short* at the same time he purchased shares in Florida Cypress Gardens. Selling HBJ stock short involved borrowing HBJ shares from a broker and selling them on the open market. An investor who sells stock short has an obligation to replace the borrowed stock at a later date. There is an old Wall Street saying that warns, "He who sells what isn't his'n, must buy it back or go to prison!" But in the arbitrageur's case it works a little differently.

An arbitrageur will generally sell short .16 of a share of HBJ (receiving $8.30) for every share of Florida Cypress Gardens he purchases at $7.50 (e.g., a sale of 800 HBJ shares for each 5000 shares of Florida Cypress Gardens purchased). If and when the merger closed, shareholders of Cypress Gardens would receive .16 of a share of HBJ stock in exchange for each of their Cypress Gardens shares: an owner of 5000 Cypress Garden shares would receive 800 shares of HBJ. The arbitrageur would then replace the borrowed HBJ stock with the HBJ shares he received in the merger. (See, he has to return the borrowed shares but, if the deal closes, he doesn't have to *buy* them back.) After the merger is successfully concluded, the arbitrageur has no stock position and a profit of eighty cents (a 50-percent annualized return!) for each share he purchased of Florida Cypress Gardens.

So, where's the bad news? This all sounds great, right?

(No doorposts around here.) Well, it seems we left out one small detail—risk. If the deal didn't go through, instead of a nice juicy eighty-cent gain, there would be a big fat $3 loss (on a $7.50 stock, yet). Hey, if HBJ ever decided to back out of the deal, maybe it would be because they discovered something seriously wrong with Cypress Gardens: The "real" Santa couldn't water-ski, the flowers were plastic, the books were cooked—you know, the usual stuff. This could mean a trading price below $4.50 and a risk much greater than $3 per share.

In this situation, though, the chance of the deal falling apart looked minimal. First, the deal seemed to make a lot of sense. Harcourt Brace owned a Sea World theme park in Orlando, not too far from Cypress Gardens. As a result, HBJ was quite familiar with running a tourist attraction and, as mentioned in some of the newspaper accounts, there seemed to be an opportunity to cross-market the two businesses. Second, there was no financing risk in the deal. Harcourt Brace was buying Cypress Gardens with common stock, and besides, relative to the size of HBJ, Cypress Gardens was a tiny acquisition, a mere blip on the radar screen. Further, there were no regulatory issues that I could see. Certainly, antitrust considerations didn't seem to be a relevant factor. And finally, as mentioned earlier, the only vote required, the one by Florida Cypress Gardens's shareholders, was in the bag.

So, what happened? Oh, nothing much. It's just that a few weeks before the deal was scheduled to close, Cypress

Gardens fell into a sinkhole. Before this happened, I really had no idea what a sinkhole was. (Apparently, in certain parts of the country, the ground unexpectedly gives way to form a big hole.) "Risk of sinkhole" was not one of my checklist items for determining whether or not to invest in a particular merger deal. The reporter from *The Wall Street Journal*, obviously not a shareholder of Cypress Gardens, seemed to find some humor in the situation. "For Florida Cypress Gardens, it was a rough day at the office," read the opening line. As it turned out, "only" the main pavilion had actually fallen into the sinkhole. According to the company's president, ". . . there was some noise, and you could see some cement blocks popping out the sides." According to *The Wall Street Journal*,

> Nobody was hurt . . . But the company said the loss of the use of the facility will likely result in a "reduction of current revenues, the extent of which is unknown as of this date."
>
> The company also said its *tentative agreement* [emphasis added] to be acquired by Harcourt Brace Jovanovich Inc. could be affected. It will take at least forty-five days to evaluate the damage and determine the extent of insurance coverage. Florida Cypress said that as a result, it expects filings made with the Securities and Exchange Commission and proxy statements related to the Harcourt merger to be delayed and perhaps revised.

I was having a few problems with all this. First off, what was this "tentative agreement" stuff all about? A deal's a deal in my book! Second, I forgot to mention another little risk. In the time between the merger announcement, when I first purchased my clever arbitrage position (buying Cypress Gardens stock, shorting stock in HBJ) and the big sinkhole fiasco, Harcourt Brace's stock had climbed to $60.75. If the deal was eventually called off, since I wouldn't be getting the HBJ stock I had expected in exchange for my Cypress Gardens shares, I would be forced to buy back the stock I had shorted in HBJ—or go to prison, remember? The added problem was, the stock I had sold for proceeds of $8.30 (.16 of a share of HBJ at 51.875) was now going to cost me $9.72 to buy back (.16 multiplied by $60.75). So, in addition to my $3 per share loss on my stock in Florida Cypress Gardens, I was going to lose an additional $1.42 (a $9.72 purchase less an $8.30 sale). That's a $4.42 loss on a $7.50 stock. But wait; if Cypress Gardens' facilities were damaged enough for the deal to be called off, maybe the stock could fall to $3.50 or even $2.50 per share. With Florida Cypress Gardens trading at $2.50, my loss would be $6.42 on a $7.50 stock. All this risk for that juicy eighty-cent profit. Somehow my warm and fuzzy feeling, my childhood memories, and my money had all fallen down the same sinkhole.

In the end, things didn't work out all that terribly. Evidently, the long-term damage to Cypress Gardens wasn't that severe. After a month of nail biting, the deal was recut from .16 share of HBJ to a fixed price of $7.90 worth of HBJ stock (based on a ten-day average price for HBJ prior to completion of the merger). The shareholder vote and close of the merger were rescheduled for mid-August. Since, at the time of the sinkhole announcement, I had to repurchase the HBJ stock I had shorted or risk further loss if HBJ continued to rise, I ended up losing the approximately $1.42 (per share of Florida Cypress Gardens purchased) that we spoke about before. I actually ended up making the forty cents between my purchase price of $7.50 and the $7.90 worth of HBJ stock I received for each share of Florida Cypress Gardens. The bottom line was that in five months, I managed to lose about $1 on my $7.50 investment. Considering what I could have lost, I was pretty relieved by the time the deal finally closed. As for my fond childhood memories . . . you can't put a price on these things—especially not a paltry $1 per share.

MORE BAD STUFF ABOUT RISK ARBITRAGE

Of course, that near disaster took place over a decade ago. Now that this sinkhole thing is on everyone's checklist, isn't it safe to get back in the water? What's wrong with just getting your feet a little wet? The truth is, things have only continued to get worse in the risk arbitrage business. Today, if the Cypress Gardens deal were announced with its original terms, instead of an eighty-cent spread, the spread would be more like thirty cents (for a compound return of 17 percent annualized). Partly this reduction is a result of lower current interest rates, but mostly it is a result of vastly increased competition in the risk arbitrage area. Don't forget, rate of return is only part of the equation. The risk/reward issue—the ratio of how much you can lose in a situation to how much you can make—is a much more important factor in determining long-term profitability. Too often, in an area that has become very competitive, this factor is overlooked in an effort to achieve what appear to be high short-term rates of return. This is especially true in fields like banking, insurance, and the stock market, where a calculator can be too easily substituted for actual thought. That's why I'm trying to lead you to investment areas which, because of the way the system works, will continue to offer extraordinary opportunities. Frankly, risk arbitrage doesn't qualify.

I may be unduly soured on the area—considering I once had seven deals break on me all at the same time—but with the constant attention required to monitor investments properly and with the other alternatives available to individuals, I believe this is an area best left alone by most investors. But if you're still not convinced . . .

CASE STUDY

Combined International/
Ryan Insurance Group

Remember the kid they used to stick out in right field? You know, the one who would always circle under the ball yelling, "I got it!—I got it!—oops, I ain't got it." Well, by the end of this next deal, I was that kid. Let me tell you, it ain't no fun.

In July 1982, Combined International agreed to acquire Ryan Insurance Group for a choice of either $34 in cash or $34 worth of Combined International stock. Under the plan, the chairman of Ryan Insurance, Patrick Ryan, was slated to become the new chief executive of the merged companies. Combined's founder, eighty-year-old W. Clement Stone, was scheduled to step down as CEO at the deal's close. The deal was subject to the signing of a definitive agreement, to approval of both companies' shareholders, and to standard regulatory approvals. Since Patrick Ryan and his family owned approximately 55 percent of Ryan Insurance group, at least one of the shareholders' votes would be easy.

The deal sailed through in record time, with a shareholder vote for each company scheduled for the end of August. Although there wasn't much of a spread in the deal (I paid about $32 for my stock), the rate of return looked attractive. After all, a $2 return on a $32 stock in two months worked out to a return of 6.25 percent. On a compounded basis, this was practically a 44-percent annualized return. Not bad, even though Ryan stock had been trading at only $18 before the deal was announced. Somehow, the 44-percent return outweighed the fact that I was trying to make only $2, while risking $14 if the deal didn't go through. While I was aware of the downside, the deal looked relatively riskless. By the time the shareholder meetings rolled around at the end of August, all the ducks were lining up nicely. (Of course, this all took place before I knew what a sinkhole was.)

Usually in an uncontested merger there's not much point in attending the special shareholder meeting. It's usually a perfunctory affair, with the outcome a foregone conclusion. That, unfortunately, is not the way W. Clement Stone saw it. Stone, best known for his philosophy of PMA ("positive mental attitude") and as a large contributor to President Nixon's campaigns, didn't feel like stepping down quietly. Apparently, according to one report from the meeting, Stone grabbed a microphone and declared that he had changed his mind, adding that "There isn't a Pat Ryan or anyone else" able to run Combined. Perhaps, Stone suggested, he should stay on as CEO. As one observer summed it up, "At the last minute, an eighty-year-old man got cold feet about giving up his company. You could see it in his face." Well, the truth is, I didn't see anything. I was sitting at my desk, pounding my glove, waiting for the ball to fall neatly into place.

The only thing I knew that afternoon, courtesy of a "friend," was that there was some sort of problem and the meeting had been adjourned. As I was working for someone else at the time and this was *my* deal, I must have turned a little green. I know this because, although I didn't say anything, my boss asked me what was wrong. You see, in the risk arbitrage business, making the $2 is no big deal. That's the way the business is supposed to work. A dollar here, two there, they all add up. Dropping $14 all at once, though,

that's a big deal. You can't have too many of those and expect to stick around too long. It could take ten more good
deals to make up for this one loss. Since I had been confi-
dently saying "I got it—I got it" for two months, this was no
time to yell "Oops!" When my boss asked me what was
wrong, I think I managed to spit out some garbled response
along the lines of "There's a little problem, but everything
will be frbljt." My stomach, on the other hand, didn't feel all
that frbljt.

In the end, Stone and Ryan were able to iron things out
and the meeting was successfully concluded later that day,
but not until after the market had closed.

Even though this deal had a happy ending, the problem
with risk arbitrage is, to borrow from Yogi Berra, "It ain't over
till it's over." Too many things have to go right too often. If you
care to spend all day playing the averages, you should be able
to earn a reasonable return on your investment. That's because, despite everything that *can* go wrong, most deals close.
But a streak of bad luck or a macroeconomic event (like a
stock-market crash or another oil shock) can send a portfolio
filled with risk arbitrage situations plummeting a lot faster,
and a lot more permanently, than a portfolio filled with special corporate situations like spinoffs. When deals fall apart,
it's always unexpected. There's just no point in putting yourself, your money, and your stomach through the hassle. If you
still want to run around the house with scissors, go ahead. But
there are easier, and safer, ways to make a buck.

Like . . .

MERGER SECURITIES

Now, here's something you *may* want to try at home—merger securities. Although cash and stock are the most common forms of payment to shareholders in a merger situation, sometimes an acquirer may use other types of securities to pay for an acquisition. These securities can include all varieties of bonds, preferred stocks, warrants, and rights. Typically, these "other" securities are used as partial payment, with the bulk of the acquisition price still being paid in cash and/or stock. In many cases, the reason merger securities are used to pay shareholders of the company being acquired is that the acquirer has already exhausted its ability to raise cash or its desire to issue additional common stock. In other cases, merger securities are used as an additional "sweetener" to clinch a deal or to outbid a potential acquirer in an auction situation.

As a general rule, no one wants merger securities. Like Rodney Dangerfield, they get no respect. Think about it. You're walking along (of course, minding your own business) when all of a sudden a takeover bid is announced for your favorite company and largest stock position, Acme Potato. Seeing great synergies in a combination of the two companies, Toppings, Inc. has just agreed to purchase each of your shares in Acme for $22 in cash and $3 in face value of Toppings 9-percent bonds due in 2010. Since shares of Acme Potato had just been trading at $16, this looks pretty good to you. But when the deal closes, what are you going to do with the proceeds? Well, you know what you're going to do with the cash—that's an easy one. You're either going to buy stock in some other company (maybe General Potato) or have a field day buying up everything at the Home Shopping Channel. But, what are you going to do with the bonds—you know, the $3-face-value of 9-percent bonds due in 2010? (These are bonds that pay interest of 9 percent on the face value of $3 until the year 2010, when bondholders receive $3 in cash.)

Well, the bonds might be a good deal. Then again they might not. The bottom line is—you couldn't care less. When you invested your money in Acme Potato, you were interested in owning stock in a potato company, or a cheap stock, or a potential takeover candidate, or all three—not in owning 9-percent bonds issued by some other company, due whenever. Well, you know what you're going to do with those bonds—you're going to sell them. You're not only going to sell them, you're going to sell them as soon as you get them. In fact, it's going to make you uncomfortable just to have that stuff, whatever it is, lying around. You're going to call your broker and shout, "Hey, I don't want these things, just get me some *real* money."

So now we know what you're going to do. But, what about the sophisticated institutions? They're going to whip out their calculators, figure out the yield to maturity for the bonds issued in the merger, compute the interest-coverage ratios and do a thorough analysis of the synergies and strategic position of the bonds' issuer, the new "spud and toppings" king. It certainly makes sense. After all, real professionals get paid to do complicated-sounding stuff like that, right? Well, whether it sounds right or not, it's not even close. They're going to sell their bonds—the same as you—only they're going to do it even faster.

Institutional investors who own stock in a potato company not only have no interest in the bonds of the new conglomerate; in most cases, they're not even *allowed* to own them. The vast majority of pension and mutual-fund managers specialize in either stock investments or bond investments. As a general rule, they're given a specific mandate to invest in one or the other, not both. Even if they can buy both stocks and bonds, it's incredibly unlikely that, out of all the available choices of bond investments, the new Toppings bonds are going to head up the list. So, in the end, practically everyone who receives merger securities, whether unsophisticated individual or sophisticated institution, is on the same page—everyone just wants out.

It should come as no surprise, then, that this is where you come in. Not unlike (in fact, incredibly similar to) the dynamics of a spinoff situation, the indiscriminate selling of merger securities, more often than not, creates a huge buying opportunity. Both spinoffs and merger securities are distributed to investors who were originally investing in something entirely different. Both spinoffs and merger securities are generally unwanted by those investors who receive them. Both spinoffs and merger securities are usually sold without regard to the investment merits. As a result, both spinoffs and merger securities (surprise, surprise) can make you a lot of money. Hopefully, by now you're starting to believe me, but just in case, let's try a few real-world examples.

CASE STUDY ✏ ✏ ✏
SUPER RITE FOODS

Did you ever want to be a big-time financier? Think you need a lot of money? Well, here's a situation where looking at merger securities turned bus fare into a ride with the big boys. The good news is that the opportunity was spelled out in readily available merger documents—only, as usual, almost no one bothered to look.

In January 1989, an investor group led by the chairman of Super Rite Foods made an offer to purchase the shares of Super Rite, a grocery chain, for $18 in cash and $5 in face amount of a newly issued preferred stock that paid dividends of seventy-five cents annually (effectively 15 percent of its face value each year). A transaction of this type, where management insiders seek to purchase all shares held by the public, is generally referred to as a *going-private* transaction. Going-private transactions are particularly interesting because these are situations where the insiders, having decided to purchase the entire equity interest in the company, are indicating a strong conviction regarding the company's future. When available, the opportunity to participate in this type of transaction through the purchase of merger securities is often worth a close look.

In this case, as reported in the newspapers, 47 percent of Super Rite was actually owned by Rite Aid Corp, the operator of a large chain of drug stores. Alex Grass, the chairman of Super Rite and the leader of the management group, also happened to be the Chairman of Rite Aid. According to Mr. Grass, since Rite Aid's board of directors was set on "liquidating its stake in Super Rite," he and his management group were interested in buying it along with the rest of the company. The management group planned to accomplish this by pursuing a *leveraged buyout* transaction. This is a technique employed in many going-private transactions, whereby a small group of investors is able to purchase a company through borrowings backed by the value of the company being acquired. Here, the management group planned to purchase all of Super Rite's shares by investing a relatively small amount of money as equity capital and borrowing the remainder of the $18 per share in cash that was being paid out to Super Rite's shareholders. In addition to paying out cash, the proposal also called for Super Rite shareholders to receive $5 in face value of new preferred stock.

The basic idea was that the future earnings of Super Rite would be able to pay the interest on the borrowings and the required dividends under the terms of the preferred stock. (This situation is analogous to the purchase of an office building: a 20-percent cash down payment is made with the remaining 80 percent of the purchase price borrowed through a mortgage; hopefully, the rent paid by the tenants will be enough to pay the principal and interest on the mortgage.) If things went well for Super Rite, the value of the original equity investment made by the management group would multiply as debt was paid down and/or the value of the business increased. One good thing about this situation was that the proxy document was going to be particularly informative. As is the case in most going-private transactions, the possibility of conflict between the interests of the management group and those of the public shareholders (including, in this instance, Rite Aid) meant that the Securities and Exchange Commission was going to take an extra hard look at the merger documents to make sure important information was adequately disclosed.

Things didn't go too smoothly for the management group, though, after the buyout announcement in January. A number of other interested parties showed up to make a bid for Super Rite, and the board of directors (minus those affiliated with the management bid) was forced to put the company up for auction. Although by March a new agreement had been reached with the same management group, this time the purchase price had been significantly increased. The winning bid for each share of Super Rite now included $25.25 in cash, $2 face-amount of a newly issued preferred stock yielding 15 percent annually, and *warrants* to buy a 10-percent interest in the new private company. Since further details about the bid weren't going to be disclosed until the proxy statement was distributed to Super Rite shareholders, at this stage there was really only one important observation to keep in mind: "Hey, they're not just paying cash for everyone's stock—they're giving out some other stuff, too. What is it?"

As a general rule, this is the same observation that should turn on the light bulb in your head whenever you read about a situation like Super Rite. Although *The Wall Street Journal* and other news publications disclose this information, they don't focus on it. That's precisely why you should. Just being aware that merger securities can provide extraordinary profit opportunities puts you at a huge advantage. While thousands of people will be reading the same headline, you will be focusing your attention and efforts in an area most people ignore. And, because almost everyone's a seller, even if more people discover your little secret, there should still be plenty of merger securities to go around. That's just the way the system works. Combine the proper focus with a little research and you can make the system work for you.

As for Super Rite, just reading some of the information provided in the proxy turned out to be an excellent road map to future profits. Distributed in August, the proxy outlined the terms of the merger, including a description of the two merger securities. Of course, the $25.25 in cash was pretty straightforward. The $2 in face value of preferred stock paying 15 percent annually (or, as the proxy called it, the "Senior Cumulative Redeemable Exchangeable Preferred Stock") was a slightly different story. What looked interesting about the preferred, though, was that each shareholder was only getting $2 face value worth for each share of Super Rite they owned. Compared to the over $25 worth of cash being paid out in the deal, the preferred would account for only a very small part of the value received by Super Rite shareholders in the buyout. This would provide a further incentive for Super Rite shareholders to simply disregard the investment merits of the preferred stock.

The other merger security, the warrants to acquire "at no cost to the holder" a 10-percent interest in the acquiring company, looked even more interesting. In general, warrants represent the right to buy stock in a company at a specified price. In this case, since the specified price was zero, warrant holders were actually stockholders in the leveraged buyout alongside management insiders. Shareholders of Super Rite were entitled to receive a set amount of warrants for each of the shares they owned in Super Rite. Since the warrants would trade publicly after the buyout was completed, anyone who wanted to participate in the leveraged buyout could simply purchase the warrants on the open market from Super Rite shareholders who chose to sell them. According to the proxy, Super Rite shareholders would receive one warrant for every 21.44 shares of Super Rite held. This fraction of a warrant, according to investment bankers hired by Super Rite, was worth between twenty-five and fifty cents per Super Rite share. If Super Rite stockholders were going to sell their preferred stock without too much thought, given the even smaller value of the warrants there appeared to be a good chance that the warrants would be sold without *any* thought.

In fact, for several months after the merger was completed, it was possible to buy the warrants very cheaply. (Each warrant gave the holder the right to purchase one share in the acquiring company formed by Super Rite management.) Since it took 21.44 shares of Super Rite to be entitled to receive one warrant, a warrant price of $6 (the approximate trading price during that period) translated to approximately twenty-eight cents worth of warrants ($6 divided by 21.44) for each share of Super Rite—hardly enough for . . . well . . . anything. Of course, $6 is what the warrants traded for, but what were they really worth? That's where reading the proxy really helped.

Under the section entitled "Certain Projections," Super Rite's management projected that in three years a new customer that Super Rite had recently obtained would be contributing over $80 million in added sales per year. According to this section of the proxy, the new entity formed by management to purchase Super Rite would be earning $5 per share in after-tax free cash flow by that time. (What's free cash flow? It's like earnings, only better. Don't get it? Don't worry—it's not hard and it's all in chapter 7.) Even at a modest multiple of ten times free cash flow per share, the new shares would be worth $50 each. That would make the warrants, the ones trading at $6, also worth $50 each (since the right to buy one share worth $50 at no cost would be worth $50). Although I am usually skeptical about long-term projections, in this case I felt that since management was buying the business they must be confident about its future. Further, even if the actual value of the business was significantly below $50 in three years, that still left a lot of room for warrant holders to walk away with a large profit. In short, buying the warrants at $6, although speculative, looked like a very good deal.

What about buying stock in Super Rite before the merger closed? I could have effectively purchased the warrants and preferred stock at an even cheaper price by buying shares in Super Rite at $25.50 or $26 in September, just before the merger closed. Since I would be getting $25.25 in cash for my Super Rite shares when the merger was completed, a $26 purchase of Super Rite would have allowed me to "create" a net purchase price of only seventy-five cents for both the $2 in face value of preferred stock *and* the warrants (or at least twenty-eight cents worth of warrants). Then again, if for some reason the deal collapsed, Super Rite might return to its predeal price of $17 or even lower. Add to that the fact that I would only be getting twenty-eight cents worth of warrants for every $26 I laid out, and the desire to pursue this option quickly faded. In the end, buying warrants (and maybe preferred stock) in the open market seemed like the best way to go.

How did it all turn out? In short, very well. Super Rite decided to go public again just two years after the merger closed. The warrants that had initially traded at $6 were valued at over $40 by the time shares in the management buyout were offered to the public. The preferred also did pretty well. While for several months after the buyout took place preferred shares could be purchased for between 50 and 60 percent of their face value, by the time the public offering was completed the preferred was worth 100 percent of face value. (This return didn't include the 15 percent in dividends payed out annually in the form of additional preferred stock.) Keep in mind, investing in the securities of a leverage buyout is generally risky business. However, it's not often that individuals have the opportunity to invest along-side management and big-time financiers. It's even more rare to be able to do so through securities that are publicly traded and available at discount prices.

Merger securities—be there—ALOHA!

CASE STUDY

PARAMOUNT COMMUNICATIONS/
VIACOM

Well, as long as everyone has a hula skirt on, let's take a look at a knock-down drag-out takeover fight that hit the front pages for nearly six months. Luckily, the fight ended in a multibillion-dollar sea of merger securities. Despite the huge amount of press the battle for Paramount Communications received, most investors missed the biggest opportunity to profit from this highly publicized situation.

In September 1993, Viacom agreed to purchase Paramount Communications for stock and cash. Viacom, a media conglomerate controlled by Sumner Redstone, was the owner of cable services (like MTV, Nickelodeon, and Showtime), cable systems, broadcast stations, and television distribution and production divisions. In what appeared to most analysts to be a good fit with Viacom, a combination with Paramount would contribute a leading producer and distributor of motion picture and television programming, a book publisher (Simon & Schuster), more cable channels, more television stations, and two sports teams. Particularly attractive to Viacom was Paramount's extensive library of past movie and television hits as well as access to the future output of Paramount's film and television studios.

Also trying to expand his media empire, Barry Diller, originator of the Fox television network and chairman of the QVC home shopping service, launched a competing bid for Paramount just one week after the Viacom announcement. After a five-month bidding war, Viacom finally prevailed, but not before significantly raising and changing the nature of its initial bid. During this period, in an effort to increase the strength of its offer, Viacom announced a merger with Block-buster Entertainment. That merger was scheduled to close shortly after the successful acquisition of Paramount. Because of the high-profile nature of all the companies involved, and the high-powered machinations of a slew of lawyers and investment bankers, the battle made interesting reading until a winner was determined in February 1994. At that time Viacom was able to purchase, for cash, 50.1 percent of Paramount's shares outstanding. Although the contest was over and the Paramount story faded from the headlines, the opportunity to profit from the merger had only begun.

The closing of the deal would not take place until after a Paramount shareholder meeting in July 1994. Since Viacom had purchased 50.1 percent of Paramount in February, the vote to approve the merger was a mere formality. What wasn't so formal was the method of payment for the remaining 49.9 percent of Paramount. While cash was the sole form of payment for purchasing the first half of Paramount's stock, practically everything *except* cash, was the form of payment for the second half of the merger—known as the back end of the merger. Mentioned but certainly not focused on in *The Wall Street Journal*, the back-end payment for each share of Paramount consisted of (1) Viacom common stock, (2) exchangeable subordinated debentures of Viacom, (3) securities known as *contingent value rights* (one for each share of Viacom common stock received in the merger), (4) three-year warrants to purchase Viacom common stock at $60 per share, and (5) five-year warrants to purchase Viacom common stock at $70 per share.

All the information about the merger and this strange collection of merger securities was provided to Paramount shareholders in a proxy statement issued in June. This information was readily available, but most shareholders had no interest in finding out what any of it meant. The vast majority of Paramount shareholders were interested in owning the shares of an entertainment conglomerate or the stock of a takeover candidate. While Viacom common stock might have been of interest to some of these shareholders, the exchangeable debentures, the contingent-value rights and the two types of warrants were going to be sold—without looking at the proxy document and without regard to their true value. Even the common stock of Viacom, the security with the best chance of being retained by Paramount shareholders, was going to come under heavy selling pressure. According to the proxy document, the Viacom stock issued to the public as part of the merger consideration would nearly triple the supply of Viacom stock in public hands.

Although the proxy was quite long, the sections outlining the merger securities were not very extensive. In fact, if you really wanted to answer the question "What is all this stuff?" a three-page section entitled "Paramount Merger Consideration" pretty well summed it up. Not surprisingly, each of the merger securities turned out to be pretty interesting.

For instance, combining the purchase of one share of Viacom common stock with the purchase of one contingent-value right (CVR) created a unique investment opportunity. The contingent-value right was a security issued by Viacom to help guarantee the value of the back-end securities that Paramount shareholders were to receive in the merger. It was probably this guarantee of value by Viacom that was responsible for its "victory" in the bidding war over Paramount. The contingent-value rights worked in the following way: If Viacom common stock traded below $48 one year after the completion of the Paramount merger, Viacom would make up the difference through a payment to holders of the CVRs. (E.g., if Viacom stock traded at $44 on the one-year anniversary of the merger's close, Viacom would pay $4 for each CVR; if Viacom traded at $38 at that time, Viacom would pay $10 for each CVR.)

By purchasing one CVR for each share of Viacom he owned, an investor could ensure that the combined value of the two securities would be at least $48 in one year. If Viacom stock traded higher than $48—let's say to $55—then, although the CVR would be worthless, the combined value of the two securities would be $55, even better than the guaranteed $48 price. Since, shortly after the merger was completed, one CVR and one share of Viacom stock could be purchased for a combined price of $37, a guaranteed price of $48 in one year looked pretty good—a 30-percent annual return with little risk and no upside limitation. Okay, there were a few little bells and whistles I left out. For one thing, Viacom limited the payout on the CVRs to a maximum of $12; even so, Viacom stock could fall to $25 before an investor who bought both the CVR and Viacom stock for a combined $37 would lose money. For another, Viacom could extend the payment date of the CVR—but only in exchange for a payout larger than $12.

Although the contingent-value rights had even more bells and whistles, beyond the specifics of this particular example, there is a larger point to keep in mind. I didn't learn about CVRs in business school. I didn't read any books that described what these things were. No one told me to buy them. I simply read the page in the proxy that told me how they worked. However, I *did* have an advantage in all this. I *did* know something that very few other investors knew. My big advantage and what I knew was this: *It pays to check out merger securities!* The takeover of Paramount provided a prime example of the kind of investment opportunities that can open up by just looking in this area. Of course, contingent-value rights weren't the only merger securities issued in the Paramount deal. A few others (actually, all the others) were worth a close look.

One of the securities, the five-year warrants to buy Viacom stock at $70 per share, looked particularly interesting. These warrants gave the holder the right to buy Viacom stock at $70 per share for a period of five years. Since Viacom stock was trading at about $32 per share in July 1994 (shortly after the Viacom warrants had been distributed to Paramount share-holders), the right to buy Viacom stock at $70 didn't look too enticing. On the other hand, with this type of situation, I like to think about the old story of the peasant who is brought before the king and sentenced to death.

The peasant says, "Oh please, please, your Majesty, spare me! If you let me live just one year, I will teach the royal horse to talk."

"Sure," responds the king, figuring what the heck, "if you can teach my horse to talk in one year, I will set you free."

On the way out of the royal palace, one of the king's guards pulls the peasant aside and asks, "Why'd you tell the king that you could make his horse talk? When the year is up, he will surely have you beheaded!"

The peasant replies, "I'm not so sure about that. A year's

an awful long time. If I have a whole year, maybe the king will change his mind. Or maybe the king will die. Maybe the horse will die. Maybe, I'll die. Or who knows? If you give him a year, maybe the horse *will* talk!"

So, if anything can happen in one year, just imagine what could happen to Viacom stock in five years! (Forget Viacom stock, imagine all the dead kings, dead peasants, and talking horses you could have!) After all, Viacom was borrowing a lot of money to finance the acquisition of Paramount. Remember, by using a lot of leverage, the value of Viacom stock could increase dramatically with an increase in the value of Viacom's assets. Also, Sumner Redstone, the owner of a majority of Viacom's common stock, was betting nearly his entire multibillion-dollar fortune on the success of the merger. Besides, ten months earlier, Viacom stock *had* traded as high as $60 per share. In addition, these were *merger securities*, bound to be trading at a cheap price. But as impressive as all this sounds, none of these reasons were the main reason why the five-year warrants to buy Viacom at $70 looked interesting.

The main reason the five-year warrants looked interesting could be found right in the three-page section describing the Paramount merger consideration. According to the proxy, the five-year warrants gave the holder the right to buy Viacom stock at any time during the next five years for $70. In the case of an ordinary warrant, this would mean that the warrant holder was entitled to receive one share of Viacom common stock in exchange for $70 in cash. But this was no ordinary warrant. In this case, the warrant holder had a choice. The

$70 could be paid in cash—and there was nothing unusual about that. However, the $70 could also be paid with $70 in face value of one of the other Paramount merger securities. Which merger security? The exchangeable subordinated debentures I mentioned earlier—item 2 on our list.

The good thing was that, shortly after the Paramount merger was completed, these merger securities were trading at 60 percent of their face value. This meant that I could buy $70 of face value of these securities for only $42 (60 percent of $70). If I also bought the five-year warrants to buy Viacom stock, under certain circumstances outlined in the proxy, I would effectively have the right to buy Viacom stock not for $70, but for only $42 worth of merger securities. I would have this right for five years. Viacom was at $32. The right to buy stock at $42 for five years was a lot more valuable than the right to buy stock at $70. If I hadn't read the portion of the proxy covering merger securities, there was no way I could have known this opportunity existed.

For anyone who still cares, there was, believe it or not, yet another twist. If the proposed merger between Viacom and Blockbuster was later completed (which it was), the terms of the warrants would change and the value of the exchangeable subordinated debentures would dramatically increase. You don't want to know the details, but the bottom line was, no matter what happened, buying both warrants and debentures was a winning trade.

Once again, although this may seem complicated, the particulars of this situation aren't relevant. The important thing is that I didn't learn any of this in school. No one told me that the Paramount merger securities had all of these weird provisions. I just knew enough to read about the merger securities in the proxy. The proxy explained how the securities worked. Most likely, the next bunch of merger securities will have totally different provisions. *Just remember to read about them.* Only invest in the ones that are attractive and that you understand. Of course, just by looking for bargains in an attractive area like merger securities, you should be way ahead of the game. Even in a high-profile takeover like Paramount, most investors didn't pay close attention to the merger securities. Since most takeovers don't make the front page for months at a time, it's no wonder that merger securities in more typical situations are completely ignored. Fortunately, most are easier to understand than the ones in the Paramount merger, but unless you make the effort to read about them, you'll miss the chance to profit from a tremendously lucrative area.

Merger securities — be there — wait, I already said that.

A QUICK SUMMARY

1. Risk arbitrage — NO!

2. Merger securities — YES!

3. The square of the hypotenuse of a right triangle is equal to the sum of the squares of the other two sides. (I threw this one in because the summary was so short.)

Chapter 5

(aka Chapter 11)

BLOOD IN THE STREETS
(HOPEFULLY, NOT YOURS)

BANKRUPTCY AND RESTRUCTURING

BANKRUPTCY

Bankruptcy, Chapter 11, el tanko, . . . th-th-that's all folks; however you say it, bankruptcy doesn't sound like the land of opportunity. The truth is that it is . . . and it isn't. The corner of the investment world occupied by companies at some stage of the bankruptcy process is filled with opportunities— and land mines. Probably the best way to approach this area, as my father might say, is with an open mind but not a hole in your head. While the securities of companies involved in one stage or another of bankruptcy are often mispriced, that doesn't necessarily mean all bankruptcy-related securities are cheap.

On the contrary, when it comes to investing in the bank- ruptcy area, picking your spots is the only way to avoid going "el tanko" yourself. After we review (and eliminate) some of the investment alternatives within the bankruptcy world, you should be able to add "picking your spots" within the bankruptcy area to your arsenal of investment weapons.

Companies end up in bankruptcy court for all sorts of reasons. A lousy business is only one of them. Some others include mismanagement, overexpansion, government regulation, product liability, and changing industry conditions. Many times, especially in the last decade, profitable, attractive businesses are forced into bankruptcy because of excessive leverage taken on as a result of a merger or leveraged buyout. In some of these cases, a business was too cyclical to make regular debt payments. In others, over-optimistic projections and too much debt combined to bankrupt an otherwise good company. It is these attractive but over-leveraged situations that create the most interesting investment opportunities.

Regardless of your opinion about the outlook for a particular business, though, it is rarely a good idea to purchase the common stock of a company that has recently filed for bankruptcy. Investors who own stock in a bankrupt company are at the bottom of the totem pole in a bankruptcy proceeding. Employees, banks, bondholders, trade creditors (mostly suppliers), and the IRS are all in line ahead of stockholders when it comes to dividing up the assets of the bankrupt company. The idea behind a bankruptcy filing under Chapter 11 of the federal bankruptcy code is to provide legal protection to a business so that it can continue operating while working out a settlement with creditors. Although bankruptcy allows a company time to restructure, even when a company does successfully emerge from this process there is seldom very much value left over for prebankruptcy shareholders. Despite this fact, the common stocks of bankrupt companies often trade at very high (and usually unjustified) valuations. This overvaluation may be due to the low dollar price of the shares, ignorance, or unwarranted speculation. The reason for this phenomenon, however, is irrelevant. The important thing to remember is that purchasing the common stock of bankrupt companies is rarely a profitable investment strategy. (Then again, if you *do* have money to burn, please feel free to run out and buy another copy of this book.)

So, if buying stock in a bankrupt company isn't the way to go, what's left to buy? The answer is—all sorts of things. First, there are the *bonds* issued by the bankrupt company. In some cases, these bonds can trade for just 20 or 30 percent of their face value. Often, a company may have several types of bonds: senior secured bonds, senior subordinated bonds, junior bonds, subordinated bonds, zero-coupon bonds, and who-knows-what bonds—all with different claims and all trading at different prices. Then, there's the bank debt. Yes, the bank debt. In the last several years a fairly vibrant market has sprung up in the defaulted bank loans of bankrupt companies. There is a whole community of brokerage firms that specialize in trading the bank debt of companies in some sort of distress. Of course, bank debt comes in different varieties, too: senior, secured, unsecured, whatever—a different flavor and a different price for each level on the bankruptcy-claim totem pole. In some situations, bank debt can also be purchased for a fraction of its original loan value.

Add to the list of actively traded bankruptcy debt—*trade*

claims. These are the claims of the bankrupt company's suppliers who didn't get paid for the goods, materials, or services they provided before the bankruptcy filing. Although the purchase and sale of trade claims is fairly complicated, many brokers who specialize in trading distressed securities also provide a marketplace for trade claims.

Unfortunately, just because you can buy the bonds, bank debt, and trade claims of bankrupt companies doesn't mean you should. During the course of a typical bankruptcy, there are all kinds of legal and financial issues that must be resolved, not only between the debtor and creditors, but between the relative claims and priorities of the different classes of creditors. The negotiations that take place are unique to the bankruptcy process and to the individual circumstances of each company. Investors who concentrate in this area, sometimes referred to as *vulture* investors, are experienced at untangling and understanding the legal and financial issues involved. In many cases, in the early stages of a bankruptcy, there is so little financial information available, and the legal and timing issues are so uncertain, that even these investors are left to make decisions with only past experience as a guide. In addition, this field, like risk arbitrage, has become very crowded in the past decade. Although there are still plenty of opportunities available to those who wish to invest in the securities of bankrupt companies, unless you are willing to make this type of specialized investing your full-time occupation it's probably best to concentrate your efforts elsewhere.

Where? Well, I'll tell you. I wouldn't waste your time talking about bankruptcy securities if I didn't have a point. Would I? Nah.

What if I told you there was a time in the bankruptcy process where all the complicated issues had been resolved? What if I told you there is a readily available public filing that pretty much sums up the outcome of the bankruptcy proceedings—complete with management's projections for the company's future operations? What if I told you that there is an opportunity to buy securities from sellers who don't want them—and never wanted them? (Remember spinoffs and merger securities? This could be déjà vu all over again!)

Well, in short, there is a time, it is available, and yes you can. While investing in the securities of a company still in bankruptcy entails all sorts of complications and risks, once a company emerges from bankruptcy, there is often an opportunity to make a new but more familiar kind of investment. Holders of the bankrupt company's debt—whether bank debt, bond debt, or trade claims—don't usually get their bankruptcy claims paid off in cash. For one thing, most companies that file for bankruptcy don't have lots of cash sloshing around. While the most senior debt holders may get some cash, usually debt holders get securities in exchange for their prebankruptcy claims—generally newly issued bonds or common stock. Therefore the new shareholders and bondholders of a company that has recently emerged from bankruptcy are, for the most part, the company's former creditors. The old shareholders, the investors who owned stock prior to the bankruptcy filing, are usually wiped out entirely or issued a few pennies' worth of warrants or common stock in the new company.

Your opportunity comes from analyzing the new common stock. Before the stock begins trading, all the information about the bankruptcy proceedings, the company's past performance, and the new capital structure are readily available in a disclosure statement. This filing is made with the bankruptcy court and can be obtained directly from the individual company, from a private document service (see chapter 7) or, under certain circumstances, from an SEC filing known as a registration statement. The disclosure statement—because it provides management's future projections for the business—actually contains more information than the registration statement filed for a more typical new stock issue. In short, the past complications of the bankruptcy proceeding are explained while the future (at least management's best cut at it) is laid out for all to see. Only many of the company's new shareholders may not care.

Since the new stock is initially issued to banks, former bondholders, and trade creditors, there is ample reason to believe that the new holders of the common stock are not interested in being long-term shareholders. Due to an unfortunate set of circumstances, these former creditors got stuck with an unwanted investment. Consequently, it makes sense that they should be anxious and willing sellers. In fact, a reasonable supposition might be that banks, bond investors, and suppliers have every reason to sell their common stock as soon as possible. While this scenario makes sense and often results in bargain opportunities, when it comes to investing in the new stock of formerly bankrupt companies, I am forced to repeat those two invaluable words of advice: Pick your spots. (*Note:* There are three kinds of people—those who can count and those who can't.)

Unlike the case of spinoffs, it is doubtful that the random purchase of stocks that have recently emerged from bankruptcy will result in a portfolio of superior long-term investments. There are probably several reasons for this. One reason is that most companies that have already spent time in bankruptcy court got there for a reason. Many are in difficult or unattractive businesses, or have uncompetitive industry positions or shrinking market niches. Many don't have the capital, even after shedding debt obligations in the bankruptcy process, to compete effectively. If a company's business were easily salable, in many cases creditors would have forced the sale while the company was still in bankruptcy. The result is that, in many instances, the quality of the companies that do come out of bankruptcy isn't all that great and the long-term performances of their stocks tend to reflect this fact (though the *real* basket cases are usually liquidated and never make it out of bankruptcy).

Nevertheless, it still stands to reason that the combination of anxious sellers and unpopular businesses should at least lead to some low initial stock prices. In fact, a study completed in 1996 by Edward Altman, Allan Eberhart, and Reena Aggarwal* found that stocks of companies emerging from bankruptcy significantly outperformed the market. For the study period of 1980 to 1993, newly distributed bankruptcy stocks outperformed the relevant market indices by over 20 percent during their first 200 days of trading. But, be careful with these statistics because it doesn't always work that way—especially in some of the larger bankruptcies. (According to the study, much of the outperformance came from the stocks with the lowest market values. It may, therefore, be difficult for large investors to duplicate these results.)

Over just the last few years, one group mentioned earlier—the vulture investors—has had an increasing effect on the bankruptcy market. These investors have tended to buy up a company's bank debt, bonds, and trade claims while the company is still in bankruptcy—before these prebankruptcy obligations are exchanged for the newly issued stock and debt. Vulture investors are betting that the new package of stock and debt will trade at a high enough price to result in a profit. Their hope is to "create" the new stock at an attractive price through the purchase of the bankrupt company's debt obligations. In some sense, then, the newly issued stock has already been "picked over by the vultures" before conventional stock investors have taken a first look.

* Edward Altman, Allan Eberhart, and Reena Aggarwal, "The Equity Performance of Firms Emerging from Bankruptcy," *New York University Salomon Center and Georgetown School of Business Working Papers*, May 1996.

So, why bother searching for bargains amidst the newly issued stocks of recently bankrupt companies? The main reason is that, notwithstanding all the circling vultures,
conditions are still ripe for these new stocks to be mispriced.
First off, these vulture investors, while well versed in the financial and legal intricacies of bankruptcy, may not have
the same time horizon or perspective as long-term value investors. Also, vultures don't usually buy up *all* the available
supply of a bankrupt company's debt securities. That leaves
banks, bondholders, and suppliers, a group not generally
looking to become stock-market heros, with an ample supply of stock—ready for sale.

Then, there's Wall Street. Unlike charitable organizations and some obscure Mongolian tribes, it doesn't work
for free. In the usual case, when a company sells its stock in
an initial public offering, armies of brokers are enlisted to
sell the new stock to their clients. Far from being drafted,
these brokers are incentivized with large sales commissions.
The brokerage firms involved in the underwriting quickly
have their research departments initiate coverage of the new
issue. Managements tour the country, on what's referred to
as a *road show*, to tout the company's prospects. By way of
contrast, Wall Street generally ignores the stocks of companies coming out of bankruptcy. No one has a vested interest
in promoting them: no commissions; no research reports;
no road show. That's why these stocks are sometimes called
orphan equities. Between the ephemeral shareholder base
and the lack of Wall Street attention, it may take quite a

while for the price of a stock issued through the bankruptcy process to accurately reflect a company's prospects.

So, if these companies are often mispriced, how can you tell the deservedly cheap ones from the real bargains? Well, one way to stay out of trouble is to follow Warren Buffett's lead and stick to good businesses. This should narrow the field substantially. As mentioned earlier, a good place to start is the category of companies that went bankrupt because they were overleveraged due to a takeover or leveraged buyout. Maybe the operating performance of a good business suffered due to a short-term problem and the company was too leveraged to stay out of bankruptcy. Maybe the earnings of a company involved in a failed leveraged buyout grew, but not as fast as initially hoped, forcing the bankruptcy filing. Sometimes companies that have made large acquisitions end up in bankruptcy simply because they wildly overpaid to acquire a "trophy" property.

Still another reason an otherwise good company may be forced to file for bankruptcy is to protect itself from product-liability lawsuits. If the liability originates from a discontinued or isolated product line, the lawsuits can usually be settled within the bankruptcy process, and a very viable company can re-emerge. Walter Industries is an example of a good company that successfully settled its asbestos liabilities in bankruptcy. Occasionally, a company may make it out of bankruptcy by shedding unprofitable business lines while banking its future on one or two profitable divisions with attractive prospects. This strategy can make a secondary, but attractive, business the main thrust of the post-bankrupt company. The hundredfold rise of the stock of Toys R Us, the surviving business that emerged from the bankruptcy of Interstate Department Stores, is the best known (and most dreamed-about) example of what can happen to an orphan stock that is created through this stategy.

Finally, if you like slumming (i.e., not following Buffett's advice), you can always choose from the just plain cheap stocks. These stocks may not be in the best or most popular businesses but, due to the dynamics of the bankruptcy process, the stock may be cheap when compared to similar companies in the same industry. The new stock of a formerly bankrupt company may be relatively undervalued because Wall Street analysts don't yet cover it, because institutions don't know about it, or simply because the company still retains a certain stigma from the bankruptcy filing. In other instances, investors may find the new capital structure, while improved, still too risky. Then again, in these cases, the substantial leverage may also allow stockholders to profit handsomely if the business performs well.

There's another reason an orphan stock may be priced cheaply—a low market value. Smaller situations may not attract vulture investors because these investors can't establish a big enough position in the bankrupt company's debt to justify the time and effort involved in doing the necessary research. The same logic applies to research analysts and institutional investors. These situations are truly orphaned and may trade cheaply for some time before they are discovered.

In the end, however, most investors would be best advised to stick to the few companies coming out of bankruptcy that have the attributes of a "good" business—companies with a strong market niche, brand name, franchise, or industry position. After all, it makes eminent sense to apply Buffett's investment concepts to a group of orphan stocks not closely followed by Wall Street.

Is everyone on board? Good. Now that I've gotten that off my chest (not to mention my conscience), let's go slumming.

CASE STUDY

CHARTER MEDICAL CORPORATION

Here's a situation where I bought into a business with uncertain prospects (sorry, Warren). I kind of knew I was treading on thin ice, it's just that the price and the upside looked so compelling, I got sucked in.

In December 1992, there were several things about the stock of Charter Medical Corporation that looked attractive. Of course, since some months earlier it had emerged from bankruptcy, it was a classic orphan equity. The stock, which had initially traded as high as $8 per share and as low as

$4.75,was trading for just over $7 when it was brought to my attention. At that price, Charter, the operator of seventy-eight psychiatric hospitals (along with ten conventional medical-surgical hospitals), seemed to be valued substantially below its competitors. The company's debt load, however, although sub-stantially reduced in the bankruptcy proceeding, was still siz-able. On the other hand, this leverage greatly increased the upside potential of Charter's stock. The other thing about the situation that looked appealing was that the insiders had a sig-nificant stake in the company through stock ownership and op-tions—and, as you already know, I kind of like that.

The problem was that Charter was operating in a very diffi-cult industry environment. Ever since 1988, when Charter was taken private through a management-led leveraged buyout, psychiatric hospitals had been under fire from insurers and managed-care providers to bring down their costs. During the four years leading to the bankruptcy filing, the average length of stay in one of Charter's hospitals (the stay lasting as long as insurers were willing to pay for it) had fallen from almost thirty days to under twenty. This put an obvious strain on revenues and cash flow. As Charter's debt had increased over a billion dollars as a result of the leveraged buyout and a major capital spending program, there was just no way that Charter was in a position to meet the interest obligations on its considerable buyout debt. When Charter filed a *prepackaged bankruptcy petition* (meaning creditors had largely agreed to the plan be-fore it was filed) in June 1992, the outlook for the industry was still uncertain. The "only" difference the bankruptcy plan made was that Charter's debt was cut to $900 million from a prebankruptcy level of $1.6 billion, the company's former creditors became the owners of new stock representing the vast majority of Charter's equity, and the stock held by the old shareholders was diluted down to a token interest in the restructured company.

It looked to me as though, based on the valuations of the most comparable hospital chains (those with large exposure in the psychiatric area), Charter should be trading closer to $15 rather than the $7 it was trading for when I finally took a look in December 1992. This discrepancy could have been because Charter had a greater exposure to the psychiatric area than some of the comparable companies I had used for comparison. Other contributing factors could have been Charter's degree of leverage, the fact that some stigma was still attached to the business from the bankruptcy, and all the reasons, in general, that an orphan stock might trade poorly—anxious sellers and little or no following on Wall Street.

None of these reasons, in my mind, justified the huge price discrepancy. According to the projections in the registration statement and the company's earnings performance for the year ended September 1992, Charter's business looked to be stabilizing. Charter's plan was to control costs, to step up marketing for new patients, and to increase its outpatient psychiatric services. It was hoped that these moves would counteract the decline in revenues caused by the trend towards shortened hospital stays. The program appeared to be well on its way. In addition, Charter stated that it was seeking to sell its group of conventional hospitals. If this happened, investor concerns about leverage might be greatly reduced. Finally, with some quick math, it appeared that Charter was going to earn between $2.50 and $3 of free cash flow per share (remember, we'll learn about free cash flow later). Even though Charter was still heavily indebted and its business was subject to the uncertainties of a changing industry, the $7 stock price looked cheap both on an absolute basis and relative to its peers.

Things went well for Charter over the next year. Costs were contained, patient admissions increased, the outpatient business continued to grow, and the conventional hospitals were sold for a good price. Also, Wall Street discovered Charter Medical—the stock tripled and I was able to sell the stock for a large gain. I may have gotten a little lucky on this one, though. If I had held on after the initial big gain, I wouldn't have made any money in Charter stock for the next three years. Perhaps there's a lesson to be learned from this poor subsequent performance.

SELLING: KNOW WHEN TO HOLD 'EM, KNOW WHEN TO FOLD 'EM

This is probably as good a time as any to discuss the other half of the investment equation—when to sell. The bad news is that selling actually makes buying look easy—buying when it's relatively cheap, buying when there's limited downside, buying when it's undiscovered, buying when insiders are incentivized, buying when you have an edge, buying when no one else wants it—buying kind of makes sense. But selling—that's a tough one. When *do* you sell? The short answer is—I don't know. I do, however, have a few tips.

One tip is that figuring out when to sell a stock that has been involved in some sort of extraordinary transaction is a lot easier than knowing when to sell the average stock. That's because the buying opportunity has a well-defined time frame. Whether you own a spinoff, a merger security, or a stock fresh out of bankruptcy there was a special event that created the buying opportunity. Hopefully, at some point after the event has transpired, the market will recognize the value that was unmasked by the extraordinary change. Once the market has reacted and/or the attributes that originally attracted you to the situation become well known, your edge may be substantially lessened. This process can take from a few weeks to a few years. The trigger to sell may be a substantial increase in the stock price or a change in the company's fundamentals (i.e., the company is doing worse than you thought).

How long should you wait before selling? There's no easy answer to that one either. However, here's a tip that has worked well for me: Trade the bad ones, invest in the good ones. No, this isn't meant to be as useless as Will Rogers's well-known advice: "Buy it and when it goes up, sell it. If it doesn't go up—don't buy it." What "trade the bad, invest in the good" means is, when you make a bargain purchase, determine what kind of company you're buying. If the company is an average company in a difficult industry and you bought it because a special corporate event created a bargain opportunity, be prepared to sell it once the stock's attributes become more widely known. In Charter Medical's case, even though the company's earnings continued strong after I bought it, I still kept in mind the difficulty and uncertainty surrounding its main business. The stock price started to reflect positive reports from Wall Street analysts and the popular press, so I sold it. No science. The stock still looked relatively cheap, but Charter was not in a business I felt comfortable investing in over the long term. The profit on the transaction (though much bigger than usual) was largely due to a bargain purchase resulting from investors' initial neglect of an orphan equity.

On the other hand, a company whose prospects and market niche I viewed more favorably, American Express, turned into a long-term investment. American Express, as you recall, was the parent company of a spinoff. It appeared to me that the unpredictability of the spinoff's business, Lehman Brothers, masked the attractiveness of the parent company's two main businesses, charge cards and financial advisory services. Purchasing these businesses at a price of nine times earnings before the spinoff took place, looked like a hidden opportunity to buy a good company at a bargain price. Because American Express owned what appeared to be good businesses, I was much more comfortable holding American Express stock for the longer term. Certainly, an extraordinary corporate change was responsible for part of my eventual profit, the spinoff creating an opportunity to make a bargain purchase. The rest of my profit, though, came because American Express's businesses continued to perform well. Eventually, the market was willing to pay an increased multiple on American Express's increasing earnings.

Under normal circumstances, I don't have the ability to spot a good business that also happens to be greatly underpriced. Warren Buffett can, but few others are in his league. By looking for bargain investment situations among those companies undergoing extraordinary corporate changes, I have a decent chance of stumbling into some good long-term investments. The bargain created or unmasked by the special corporate event—that's what draws me in. The quality and nature of the business—that's what usually determines how long I stay. So trade the bad ones, invest in the good ones. If you combine this tidbit with Will Rogers's advice, there's no telling how far you could go.

CORPORATE RESTRUCTURING

Corporate restructuring is another area where extraordinary changes, ones that don't always occur under the best of circumstances, can create investment opportunities. While the term "corporate restructuring" can mean a lot of things, when *we* talk about restructuring, we won't be talking about minor tweaking around the edges, we'll be talking about *big* changes. This means the sale or shuttering of an entire division. Not just any division, either. We're talking a *big* division, at least big in relation to the size of the entire company.

Of course, corporate restructurings are going on all the time. It's a painful and sometimes necessary part of the capitalist system. The type of restructuring situations that we'll focus on and the ones that provide the most clear-cut investment opportunities are the situations where companies sell or close major divisions to stanch losses, pay off debt, or focus on more promising lines of business.

The reason why major corporate restructurings may be a fruitful place to seek out investment opportunities is that oftentimes the division being sold or liquidated has actually served to hide the value inherent in the company's other businesses. A simple example might be a conglomerate that earns $2 per share and whose stock trades at thirteen times earnings, or $26. In reality, that $2 in earnings may really be made up of the earnings of two business lines and the losses of another. If the two profitable divisions are actually earning $3 per share while the other division contributes a $1 loss, therein lies an opportunity. If the money-losing division could simply be sold or liquidated with no net liability, the conglomerate would immediately increase its earnings to $3 per share. At a price of $26, this would lower the stock's earnings multiple from thirteen to less than nine. In many cases, the sale or liquidation of a loss-ridden business can result in positive net proceeds. Of course, this would make the investment opportunity more compelling.

Similar to the benefits that result from spinoffs, the sale of a major division may create a more focused enterprise which can offer real advantages to both the company and its shareholders. This benefits both management—who can focus on more limited and promising operations—and the value of the company in the marketplace—which may be willing to pay a premium for more specialized and profitable business operations. Though it may seem counterintuitive (because, in many such cases, there has been a business failure), companies that pursue a major restructuring are often among the most shareholder oriented. Unless a company is in extreme distress, just making the decision to sell a major division is an extremely difficult thing to do. Most managements that go through with such a plan have their eye on shareholder interests.

There are basically two ways to take advantage of a corporate restructuring. One way is to invest in a situation *after* a major restructuring has already been announced. There is often ample opportunity to profit after an announcement is made because of the unique nature of the transaction. It may take some time for the marketplace to fully understand the ramifications of such a significant move. Generally, the smaller the market capitalization of a company (and consequently the fewer the analysts and institutions following the situation), the more time and opportunity you may have to take advantage of a restructuring announcement.

The other way to profit is from investing in a company that is ripe for restructuring. This is much more difficult to do. I don't usually seek out these situations, although sometimes an opportunity can just fall in your lap. The important thing is to learn how to recognize a potential restructuring candidate when you see one. If it's obvious to you, many managements (especially those with large stock positions) are often thinking along the same lines.

At least, that's what happened in this next case.

CASE STUDY
GREENMAN BROTHERS

For this one, I have to give credit where credit is due. First to my wife, who alertly discovered the opportunity, and next to Peter Lynch, who planted the seed.

While I'm always trying to get my wife, a full-time mother and sometime attorney, hooked on the stock market, I didn't know what progress I was making until she came home one day having completed a good piece of investigative work. Not far from our home, my wife had discovered a new store that specialized in educational toys and crafts for children. She was so impressed with the concept and the atmosphere of the store that she asked the store manager (a Peter Lynch suggestion which she had apparently taken to heart) whether the store, "Noodle Kidoodle," was owned by a public company. The answer: Yes, it was owned by Greenman Brothers, traded on the American Stock Exchange. In the middle of her recounting of the story, I had to make her stop for a moment. I told her the tears were beginning to well up and that I needed a tissue. Naturally, I was only (half) joking.

Upon further investigation (after all, how many hot tips can I expect from my wife?), Greenman turned out to be a marginally profitable distributor of toys, housewares, and stationery. In effect, Greenman was the middleman between manufacturers and over 7,000 retail stores. The Noodle Kidoodle stores were a new venture for the company; the division expected to grow substantially if the first stores proved successful. It certainly looked to me as if the concept had a lot of promise. When I visited the same store my wife had initially seen, the displays, the unique merchandise, and the crowds seemed to shout "Hey, this place is great!" I couldn't see any reason why, if the concept worked for five or ten local stores, the whole country couldn't be covered by a hundred, two hundred, or even more stores. This is precisely the type of retail concept that Peter Lynch had said to keep an eye out for—and because of my wife, I was in on the ground floor!

Ordinarily, with this type of opportunity, I don't care what I think. What a great concept! What a fantastic new product! This could be a home run! These are thoughts I have from time to time, but I do my darnedest to ignore them. Whenever you can buy into one of these great new concepts or products through the stock market, there's usually a price tag that goes along with it. The stock price could be twenty, thirty, or fifty times earnings. In many cases, the price/earnings ratio could be infinite — in other words, the business is so new, there are no earnings; in the case of "concepts," there may be no sales, either! My negative attitude toward investing in fast-growing (or potentially fast-growing), high-multiple stocks will probably keep me from investing in the next Microsoft or Wal-Mart. But I figure, since I'm no wizard at forecasting the next big retail or technological trend, I'll probably miss out on a pile of losers, too. For me, this is a fair trade-off because (as I've pointed out before) if you don't lose, most of the other alternatives are good.

So, what the heck was I doing in the middle of Noodle Kidoodle contemplating a big investment in Greenman Brothers? Was I merely placating my wife (a usually wise if not always profitable strategy)? Not at all. Greenman, as I had learned earlier, was mainly in the distribution business. While this business wasn't earning much money, the good news was that the stock was trading just above $5, yet Greenman had a book value of over $8 per share. Not that book value — the value of Greenman's assets (based on historical cost) less all liabilities — was the only measure of the stock's value. After all, if Greenman couldn't earn much money with those assets, what were they really worth? It's just that being a wholesale distributor, a middleman between manufacturers and retailers, Greenman didn't need much in the way of fixed assets like plant and equipment. Most of Greenman's assets were in cash, receivables, and recently purchased inventory—the type of assets that, under most circumstances, could be readily sold.

The way my thinking went, this dull and barely profitable distribution business was masking the potential of a great new retailing concept. With Greenman selling for less than $6 per share, it didn't seem that the market was giving any value at all to the prospects for Noodle Kidoodle. Since Greenman had already disclosed its plans to greatly expand the chain (assuming the continued success of the initial stores), the new retail business could eventually dwarf the potential and profits of the distribution business. The problem was, even if I was right about the vast potential, an expansion of the magnitude I was hoping for would cost money. Since Greenman had almost no debt, borrowings could be one source of funds. I figured another source of funds could be the distribution business: If Noodle Kidoodle ended up panning out, maybe Greenman could sell its distribution business. Even a 25-percent haircut to the $8 book value of Greenman's assets would yield proceeds of $6. A haircut of 40 percent would still mean I was paying next to nothing for a business I was extremely excited about.

But wait a second. I already said I don't feel comfortable investing in these new-concept, high-growth companies. Well, actually, what I really said was—I hate losing money on these things. I'm always worried that paying big multiples to earnings (or sales) based on my own future growth projections could lead to big losses. That's the kind of investing that makes me uncomfortable. Here, at a price under $6, I wasn't paying anything for what I considered to be Noodle Kidoodle's vast potential. From what I had seen, the new chain had success written all over it—and since I was making the bet for free, the price was right.

Of course, the enthusiasm over Noodle Kidoodle's first stores could fizzle, the chain could run into competition or the trend toward educational toys could be a local phenomenon or a passing fad. But since I wasn't really paying much, if anything, for the business, I probably wasn't going to lose much if things went sour. The risk that Greenman's distribution business would take a dramatic turn for the worse didn't bother me much, either. Although that business wasn't losing money, if it started to, given the salable nature of its assets, maybe Greenman would exit distribution and concentrate on Noodle Kidoodle. Any way I sliced it, with the price I was paying, there weren't too many scenarios that ended in a big loss. The upside? I wasn't sure, but "oodles" was a definite possibility.

What happened? Well, the stock went nowhere for a little over a year, trading as high as $7 per share and as low as $4. During this time, Noodle Kidoodle's stores continued to do well and Greenman announced plans to open an additional fifteen stores, making a total of twenty by the end of 1995. On the other hand, the distribution business only got worse. By May 1995, more than a year after my initial purchase, the stock was still trading below $6 per share. It was at that time that Greenman made an announcement: it was investigating the possible sale of its wholesale distribution business. In a press release, Greenman said a sale would "free up capital that will be needed to grow our Noodle Kidoodle retail business," which it planned to expand. All of a sudden, Greenman was no longer a stodgy, slow-growing distributor but a fast-growing retail dynamo. The stock moved to $11 in two months and to $14 within four months. I sold my stock between $10 and $11.

Hey, call me chicken, but I had to sell. Greenman had become a hot stock. I wasn't getting anything for free anymore—and besides, what the heck did I know about high flyers? Plenty could still go wrong. It was going to take a lot more than twenty Noodle Kidoodle stores before Greenman would become profitable. Who knew what havoc fickle shoppers and competition could wreak on a fledgling toy chain? In short, the price jump had turned Greenman into the kind of stock I'm just not comfortable owning. A corporate restructuring had unleashed the hidden value that I had originally seen, the story was out, and my initial advantage was gone.

You could say I got a little lucky here. Management could have taken longer to restructure the business or there might have been no restructuring at all. If I invested in every company that *might* restructure, I could be waiting forever—and my investment returns, while I waited, probably wouldn't be all that great. The Greenman situation, however, had three qualities that made it particularly attractive. Limited down-side was clearly one. We've probably beaten that concept to death—but so what; "margin of safety" should always top your investment list. The next feature Greenman had was a business to restructure around. In this case, if the distribution business was sold, Noodle Kidoodle would remain as a vi-able and attractive business. The third feature the Green-man situation had was some sort of catalyst to set things in motion. Greenman had hit on a hot new concept that, if suc-cessful, was going to require substantial funding. If Noodle Kidoodle took off, Greenman was going to need money from somewhere. The fact that the distribution business contin-ued to deteriorate probably made the decision to restructure by seeking a buyer for the business that much easier.

In the end, setting out to find *potential* restructuring candi-dates presents a difficult challenge. I don't think this would be a fruitful exercise for most investors. On the other hand, "to know one when you see one" is the kind of prospecting everyone can do. Just make sure that the business that ini-tially piques your interest is large enough relative to the whole company to make a real difference. Although these opportunities are few and far between, you can make a lot of money by spotting an attractive business before it has been uncovered through a restructuring.

Of course, when a company comes right out and tells you they plan to restructure, that's a situation much easier to spot. That's why most of your restructuring opportunities will fall into this category. Even after a restructuring is announced, there's often plenty of time to do research and profit. In fact, I only became involved in this next restructuring after the stock had nearly tripled. Fortunately, there was still plenty of profit left for the slowpokes.

CASE STUDY
GENERAL DYNAMICS

The first time I noticed General Dynamics was in June 1992. *The Wall Street Journal* reported that the company, a major defense contractor, planned to buy back 13,000,000 of its own shares from shareholders. This amount equalled 30 percent of General Dynamics's total shares outstanding. The offer to buy shares was to be accomplished through something known as a *dutch auction tender*. In this offer, shareholders were offered the chance to tender their shares back to the company at a price between $65.375 and $75. Based on how many shares were tendered and at what prices, General Dynamics would set a single price that enabled it to buy back up to the 13 million shares. All shares that had been tendered at or below the set price would be purchased at that price under the offer.

When I looked at the offer and read about the transaction and its background, the particular details of how the stock was going to be repurchased didn't seem all that important. The thing that struck me, after reading through the newspaper accounts and the tender documents (filed with the SEC), was the overall plan General Dynamics had set in motion over a year earlier. As a consequence of shrinking defense budgets, a process that looked to be accelerating with the collapse of the Soviet Union, General Dynamics had decided to drastically revise its operating philosophy. Under the leadership of William Anders, a former Apollo astronaut, the company had embarked on a major restructuring plan to focus on selected core businesses. At the start of the new program, in February 1991, a stock incentive plan for twenty-three top executives was instituted. At that time, General Dynamics's stock stood at approximately $25 per share. By the time I first looked at the stock, after the announcement of the Dutch auction tender in June 1992, the stock had risen to $71; the company's shareholders had already made a fortune and the stock's dramatic rise had left the company's top executives with well over $20 million in profits.

After seeing that, why didn't I just walk away? I was clearly late to the party—no, more than late; shareholders had had their dessert, maybe even seconds and thirds. So, what made me look further? Well, one thing smack on the front page of the tender document was an encouraging sign. It was a disclosure about the level of participation by the management shareholders in the company's buyback offer. Even after enjoying a spectacular rise in the value of their shares, management wasn't selling *any* stock back to the company in the Dutch auction tender. This was an indication to me that the insiders, the people most familiar with the company's prospects, thought the stock was still undervalued. If, indeed, the stock *was* undervalued at the buyback price, the results could be dramatic. Simple math indicated that repurchasing a huge chunk of stock below its true value would result in a windfall for those stockholders who retained their shares. Additionally, future increases in the company's value would be magnified over the smaller amount of shares that remained outstanding.

A further sign of encouragement came from the restructuring plan itself. Not only did it appear to make good sense, but despite the substantial progress made thus far, it was nowhere near completed. According to the tender document, under the heading "Background and Business Strategy," General Dynamics had a well-defined game plan. It was management's "belief that the defense industry (would) have to eliminate substantial overcapacity if it (was) to provide the United States with a viable defense industrial base. Therefore, it was determined that only those businesses with leadership in their markets could remain effective once the rationalization of the industry was substantially complete." Under that principle, General Dynamics had selected four core businesses on which to pin its future. The company planned to "continually investigate ways to strengthen" each of these businesses "by possible combination with others, the formation of ventures to eliminate excess facilities, the acquisition of a compatible business, or, if appropriate, the sale of a business." All of General Dynamics's remaining businesses, those considered "noncore," were to be sold under the plan.

In essence, General Dynamics was going to be looking at restructuring opportunities for a long time to come—both in its noncore businesses, which were clearly going to be sold, and in its core businesses, which were going to be continually restructured. Already, over the previous year, General Dynamics had sold its computer operations and a large subsidiary, the Cessna Aircraft Company, for proceeds of nearly $800 million. Also, in just the previous month, the company had announced the sale of its missile business, expected to net an additional $450 million. According to the tender document, the timetable for selling the remaining "noncore" businesses called for completion of the entire process before the end of 1993. Proceeds from the sales were to be distributed to General Dynamics's shareholders. In addition, since the businesses to be sold represented well over 20 percent of the company's total business, under the tax code shareholders would receive favorable tax treatment on the distributions.

Which brings us to the last reason I was interested in the General Dynamics situation. Notwithstanding how late I was to the restructuring and regardless of how far the shares had already risen, the stock still looked cheap. All told, even after spending $950 million buying back shares in the tender offer and excluding any future earnings, it looked as though General Dynamics was going to end up with well over $1 billion in cash to return to shareholders—or to spend solidifying the market position of its core businesses. Subtracting the expected cash proceeds from the stock price left me with a net price for General Dynamics's remaining core businesses. Even using conservative estimates, this price meant that I was "creating" General Dynamics's continuing businesses at a 40-percent discount to the other defense contractors. Given the focused nature of the company's disposal program, and the fact that management planned to continue restructuring even the core businesses, I didn't think that the discount could last for very long. The company's track record and management's incentive program gave me a high degree of confidence that the market would eventually give full credit to the values being uncovered through the restructuring plan.

What happened? Things worked out better than I had ever hoped. In the beginning of July 1992, the company repurchased the 13,000,000 shares at a price of $72.25, reducing the shares outstanding to under 30,000,000. Just two weeks later, an event that would warm any shareholder's heart took place: Warren Buffett announced that he had acquired over 4,000,000 shares, or approximately 15 percent, of General Dynamics. (See, you *are* in good company, sometimes even Buffett gets attracted to these special corporate situations.) Despite this seal of approval from the world's greatest investor, there was still plenty of time to purchase General Dynamics stock as it traded between $75 and $80 for almost two months after the Buffett announcement. As it turned out, this would have been a good move.

Sales of noncore businesses continued, and in December

1992, General Dynamics announced the sale of one of its core businesses, the tactical-aircraft division, for over $1.5 billion. Although this division was one of the company's selected core businesses, the sale was in line with General Dynamics' overall plan disclosed in the tender document: "to continually investigate ways to strengthen" each of its core businesses "by possible . . . acquisition of a compatible business . . . or, the sale of a business." Over the following year, after each sale and dividend distribution announcement, I reassessed my initial valuation work. At each step, the values and the operating performance of the remaining businesses continued to improve. By the end of 1993, General Dynamics's restructuring process had resulted in dividend distributions of over $50 per share and a stock price, even after the distributions, of over $90 per share. This total of over $140 meant that the stock had more than doubled in less than eighteen months—and it had all happened *after* I read about the company's tender offer in the paper.

Yes, I was late to the party. But, in this case, better late than never. Of course, not all restructurings work out quite this well. It's pretty amazing when a change in strategic outlook (along with some favorable market conditions) can change the market's valuation of the same set of businesses from $25 per share to more than $140 per share in under three years. On the other hand, in recent years, managements have been feeling the pressure to make their operations more focused, and consequently more understandable, to the investment community. Reports of another corporation's decision to restructure through the spinoff or sale of an unrelated business, are an everyday occurrence. The experience of General Dynamics and its shareholders is merely an extreme example of the type of hidden value that can be unleashed through this process.

A Quick Summary

1. **Bankruptcy—some points to remember**
   a. Bankruptcies can create unique investment opportunities—but be choosy.
   b. As a general rule, don't buy the common stock of a bankrupt company.
   c. The bonds, bank debt, and trade claims of bankrupt companies can make attractive investments—but first—quit your day job.
   d. Searching among the newly issued stocks of companies emerging from bankruptcy can be worthwhile; just like spinoffs and merger securities, bargains are often created by anxious sellers who never wanted the stuff in the first place.
   e. Unless the price is irresistible, invest in companies with attractive businesses—or as Damon Runyon put it,
      "It may be that the race is not always to the swift nor the battle to the strong—but that is the way to bet."

2. **Selling Tips**
   a. Trade the bad ones; invest in the good ones.

b. Remember that hypotenuse thing from the last chapter—it won't tell you when to sell, but at least I'm sure it's right.

3. **Restructuring**

   a. Tremendous values can be uncovered through corporate restructurings.

   b. Look for situations that have limited downside, an attractive business to restructure around, and a well-incentivized management team.

   c. In *potential* restructuring situations, also look for a catalyst to set things in motion.

   d. Make sure the magnitude of the restructuring is significant relative to the size of the total company.

   e. Listen to your spouse. (Following this advice won't guarantee capital gains, but the dividends are a sure thing.)

Chapter 6

"Baby Needs New Shoes"
Meets
"Other People's Money"

Recapitalizations and Stub Stocks,
Leaps, Warrants, and Options

Okay. So I told you about spinoffs in chapter 3. That information alone was worth the price of this book. Throw in chapters 4 and 5—merger securities, bankruptcies and restructurings—and we're talking at least a $60 value. And now, you ingrate, you want even more! More risk, more reward, more money!

Well, fine. I'll help you out. But, frankly, you're not the type of person I really care to associate with, and if you're expecting me to throw in a set of Ginsu knives—you can just forget it.

RECAPITALIZATIONS AND STUB STOCKS

One way a company can create value for its shareholders is to recapitalize its balance sheet. For a period in the 1980s, *recaps*, as they are known on Wall Street, were a popular way for companies to ward off the advances of a hostile takeover artist or to placate restive shareholders. Generally, in a *recapitalization* transaction, a company repurchases a large portion of its own common stock in exchange for cash, bonds, or preferred stock. Alternatively, cash and/or securities can be distributed directly to shareholders through a dividend. The result of a recapitalization is usually a highly leveraged company that is still owned by the original shareholders. Even though recaps are not as popular as they once were (due to the large number of excessively leveraged companies that filed for bankruptcy in the late 1980s and early 1990s), there's still a good reason to learn about them. But, we'll get to that later.

First let's see how a recap works. Let's assume that XYZ Corporation is trading at $36 per share. Deciding that a recapitalization transaction will be good for shareholders, the company decides to distribute $30 worth of newly issued bonds to its own shareholders. Theoretically, if XYZ stock was worth $36 before it distributed $30 of value to its shareholders, then after the distribution, the market should value the common stock at approximately $6 per share—and if that was all that happened, recaps would be no big deal. But it's not that simple.

In practice, recaps tend to create additional value for shareholders for a number of reasons. One reason is that there is a tax advantage to having a leveraged balance sheet. Let's assume that, prior to the recap, XYZ earned $3 per share after taxes—for a price/earnings ratio of 12 based on its $36 stock price. The tax rate, including state taxes, is assumed to be 40 percent, so pretax earnings for XYZ are actually $5 per share ($5 in pretax earnings less $2 in taxes equals our $3 per share in after-tax earnings). Now let's see what happens when we leverage up the balance sheet through the recap.

If the $30 of bonds distributed to shareholders carry an interest rate of 10 percent, then XYZ will owe $3 in interest on the bonds each year. Since interest is a tax-deductible expense for corporations, the new pretax earnings for XYZ Corporation will now come to $2 per share (the $5 of previous pretax earnings less the $3 per share in interest expense). Assuming the same 40-percent tax rate, this $2 in pretax earnings will net out to $1.20 per share after tax. Thus, if the common stock of XYZ after the recap (usually referred to as the *stub stock*) were to trade at only $6, the price/earnings ratio would be down to 5. That's usually much too low.

Of course, the stub stock probably doesn't deserve the same twelve-times-earnings multiple that XYZ commanded before the recap. After all, the greatly increased debt load raises the risk to investors in XYZ common stock—and since investors like to get paid for taking on additional risk, the stub stock *should* trade at a lower earnings multiple. How low? It's no science, but a new price/earnings ratio of 8 or 9 wouldn't seem unreasonable. This would leave the stub stock trading at around $10 (for a P/E of 8.33), resulting in a total value for the recap package of about $40 per share ($30 in debt plus a $10 stub) versus the original pre-recap price of $36.

Does this result make sense? XYZ's assets haven't changed. The sales and earnings power of the business are the same. Where does the $4 gain to shareholders come from, anyway? Isn't this recap stuff just a bunch of smoke and mirrors? You know, what they call financial engineering? Well, not really.

The trick is in the taxes. Before the recap, of the $5 in pre-tax earnings $3 went to shareholders in the form of earnings and $2 went to Uncle Sam in the form of taxes. After the recap, $3 goes to shareholders in the form of interest payments on the newly distributed bonds and an additional $1.20 goes to shareholders in the form of earnings on the stub stock. That's a total of $4.20 going to shareholders versus just $3 before the recap. Uncle Sam's cut, as a result of the recap, is just $0.80—down from $2 before the recap took place. No smoke and mirrors. Leveraging the balance sheet (but not overleveraging it) just turns out to be a more tax-effective way to distribute earnings to shareholders—and that's definitely worth something.

Of course, you're not going to hear about the recap until after it's already been announced in the papers. So much of the $4 gain created by the recapitalization transaction will already be reflected in XYZ's stock price before you get a chance to invest. Still, recaps can provide ample opportunity to profit. For instance, in recap situations where debt or preferred securities are distributed directly to shareholders, the profit opportunities can be similar to those available through investing in merger securities. Investors who owned the common stock of XYZ generally don't want the company's debt and preferred securities. Consequently, shortly after being distributed these newly issued securities are often sold indiscriminately. But, you know this story already— and anyway, it's the other part of the recap story that can get really exciting.

That part involves investing in the stub stock—the equity stake that remains after the company has been recapitalized. This is where you can make the big money. Essentially, investing in a stub stock is just like investing in the equity portion of a publicly traded leveraged buyout. Many leveraged buyouts have returned five or ten times the original equity investment, and several stub stocks have produced similarly spectacular returns. Sure, leveraged buyouts have been known to fail, and likewise, the value of some stub stocks has vaporized—but the payoffs on the ones that *do* work can more than make up for a few losers. In fact, there is almost no other area of the stock market where research can be rewarded as quickly and as generously as in the careful analysis of stub stocks.

Why can stub stock investing be so lucrative? The answer is pretty straightforward: it's all in the numbers. While we have previously discussed the various benefits and risks of investing in leveraged companies, reviewing the math, once again, can only help to highlight the opportunity. In our example, let's assume that XYZ's pretax earnings improve 20 percent, increasing from $5 per share to $6. Assuming no recap, a 40-percent tax rate will take after-tax earnings to $3.60 per share. At a multiple of 12 times earnings, XYZ stock will move from $36 to $43.20 per share, for an increase of 20 percent.

Assuming XYZ goes through with the recap, the story looks a little different. Using the assumed increase in pretax earnings to $6, and subtracting the $3 of interest payable on the bonds distributed in the recapitalization, we come out with $3 in taxable income. After paying 40 percent in taxes, the after-tax earnings of XYZ's stub stock work out to $1.80 per share. Using the same multiple as earlier (8.33 times earnings), XYZ's stub stock is now worth $15—up 50 percent from the original stub price of $10. Taking it a step further, now that XYZ's pretax earnings exceed its interest expense even more comfortably than in the original scenario, the stock may be viewed as less risky. A price/earnings ratio of 10 might now seem reasonable. Therefore, the stub stock could actually trade to $18 per share (10 times $1.80 in earnings), or an 80-percent gain from the original $10 price. Once again, this potential 80-percent gain was made possible by a relatively modest 20-percent increase in pretax earnings. As you can imagine, *when they work*, leveraged recaps can be both fun and profitable.

Unfortunately, as I mentioned earlier, nowadays investors don't have many opportunities to invest in the stub stocks of recapitalized companies. For the moment, at least, recaps are out of fashion. However, if the idea of investing in leveraged equities still excites you, I do have two suggestions. First, investing in leveraged spinoffs can give you every bit as much bang for your buck as investing in stub stocks—and there's absolutely nothing wrong with looking very closely at this area, except that we've already covered it. The second suggestion is what I promised you at the start of the chapter: a way to use what you've learned about recaps to your advantage. Since, for the most part, companies are no longer pursuing the recap route themselves, it's a way for you to create your own recap (sort of).

But, before we get to that, let's go back to the heyday of recaps, the mid-1980s, to see how one works in real life.

CASE STUDY

FMC CORPORATION

In February 1986, FMC Corporation, a defense contractor and manufacturer of chemicals and machinery, announced plans to pursue a major recapitalization. FMC's move was prompted by concerns that the company was being stalked by a hostile suitor. After reviewing the available alternatives, FMC's board of directors decided that a recap was the best way to fend off a potential takeover. It was hoped that the recap would both boost the company's stock price and give the company's management and employees a greater equity stake in the ongoing enterprise. If the recap was successful, a hostile bidder would be deterred and management and employees would retain control over their own destiny.

Under the plan, for each share held FMC shareholders were to receive a cash distribution of $70 as well as one new share in the recapitalized company. In lieu of the cash payment, management shareholders and shareholders in the company's employee stock plan were to receive additional shares in the recapitalized company. So instead of receiving $70 in cash, management shareholders would receive an additional 4⅔ shares of the recapitalized company. This meant that management would receive a total of 5⅔ shares of the recapitalized stub stock for each FMC share held before the recap. After the plan was completed, insider ownership in FMC would increase from 19 percent to over 40 percent of the company's shares.

At first the plan appeared to have the desired effect. FMC stock, which had been trading at around $70 before takeover rumors began circling around the company, moved to approximately $85 per share after the recapitalization plan was announced. This implied that the market was placing a value of approximately $15 on the stub stock that would remain after the $70 distribution was made to outside shareholders. Takeover rumors did not abate, however, and the stock continued to climb into the mid-$90s over the next six weeks. In early April, Ivan Boesky, the infamous takeover trader and sometime corporate raider, announced that he had purchased a 7.5-percent stake in FMC's shares outstanding. He announced that, in his opinion, the recapitalization plan was too generous to management shareholders and that he planned to oppose the plan when it came up for a shareholder vote the following month.

Partially in response to Boesky's opposition to the plan, as well as to the significant increase in the company's stock price, the company announced an amendment to the plan several weeks later. Citing "current economic and market conditions which reflect declining interest rates and strong market interest in the plan," FMC increased the amount of the cash distribution to $80 per share. Despite the increased payment to outside holders, the number of stub shares that management and employees were to receive was to remain the same as originally proposed under the initial plan. A proxy statement describing the revised recapitalization plan was filed with the SEC in early May 1986 with a shareholder vote scheduled for later that month.

Since I knew that stub stocks can often produce spectacular gains, I read the proxy material with much interest. What caught my eye was a prominent part of the proxy entitled "Certain Projections." In this section, management had laid out its best guess as to what FMC's income statement, cash flow, and balance sheet would look like for the next eight years. As I've mentioned before, I take management projections with a grain of salt. Long-range projections are even more suspect. But in this case, I paid a little more attention. After all, management wasn't taking any cash from the recapitalization; they were forgoing an $80 cash dividend in exchange for a larger equity stake in the recapitalized company. Not only that but, more than ever, FMC's managers would be betting their fortunes and careers on the success of the company going forward.

211

According to the projections, in just three years FMC was expected to earn $3.75 per share—with after-tax free cash flow of approximately $4.75 per share. By that time, the company's pretax earnings were anticipated to exceed its annual interest expense by a ratio of almost 2 to 1—and at a multiple of perhaps 10 times free cash flow, the stub stock could be approaching $50 per share. With FMC trading at approximately $97 per share (and assuming the recapitalization was successful), this meant that I could create the stub stock at a price of $17 ($97 stock price less the $80 cash distribution). If FMC's projections came close to being correct, this would turn out to be a real bargain.

What happened? The stock hit $40 about a year after the recap was completed and briefly touched $60 several months later just before the crash in October 1987. However, to prove the old adage that leverage works both ways (i.e., big upside potential and big downside risk), the stock fell all the way back to $25 in the aftermath of the crash before settling in at around $35. What happened to me? I missed all the action. For some reason that I can't recall, I sold my position in FMC at about $26 several months after the recapitalization was completed. Maybe I wasn't enamored with the quality of FMC's businesses and just followed my own advice by "trading the bad ones" (or maybe I got up on the wrong side of bed the day I decided to sell). Regardless, I was kind of glad to miss out on that kind of "fun."

Oh yes. I almost forgot. As it turned out, Boesky had acquired his original position in FMC based on inside information. The company later sued him for forcing the $10 dividend increase under the recap plan. After admitting to many instances of securities fraud (including a rather sophisticated scheme where he exchanged suitcases loaded with cash for inside tips), Boesky was sentenced to several years in prison. In the end, Boesky did his time—and, if you've read this far, so have you. That's why I'm finally going to tell you how to put your knowledge of stub stocks and their explosive profit potential to good use.

LEAPS (LONG-TERM EQUITY ANTICIPATION SECURITIES)

As I mentioned earlier, there is a way to create your own version of a stub stock. Simply by choosing among the hundreds of available LEAPS, you can create an investment situation that has many of the risk/reward characteristics of an investment in the leveraged equity of a recapitalized company. The term LEAPS is nothing more than an acronym for a long-term option contract (Long-term Equity AnticiPation Security). If you're thinking "That's great, but what's an option?" don't sweat it too much. While there are two kinds of options—puts and calls—we'll only be talking about the calls. Further, we'll only be talking about the kind of calls that trade on a national securities exchange—*listed calls*. (All right. So that didn't make you feel any better. But read on anyway; there's big money at stake.)

A *call* is merely the right—but not the obligation—to buy a stock at a specified price for a limited period of time. So a June call to buy IBM at $140 per share gives the owner of the call the right to buy IBM at a price of $140 per share until the call expires in June (the third Friday of each month is considered the expiration date for listed options). If at the expiration date IBM stock is trading at $148, the call would be worth $8. This is because the right to buy stock at $140, when the stock can be immediately resold for $148, is worth $8. If, on the other hand, IBM stock is trading at only $135 on the call's expiration date, then the call expires worthless. This is because the right to buy stock at $140 (usually referred to as the *strike* or *exercise price*) isn't worth anything if everyone can just go out into the marketplace and purchase the same stock for $135. Well, that just about covers the basics—except there's one more step.

Pretty much whenever the stock market is open, the options market is also open. There aren't listed options available for every stock that trades, but options do trade on thousands of the largest companies. Therefore, if a stock has listed calls, you can usually buy and sell them during market hours up until their respective expiration date. In our example, the June $140 calls to buy IBM stock were trading for months prior to their June expiration. We've already discussed what the call would be worth on its expiration date. The question is: What is the fair value of the call before the expiration date? To be more specific, how much should you pay for the calls if you buy them in April, approximately two months before they expire? (While you don't really have to figure out the correct pricing for a call, it *is* good to understand where the price comes from. *Note:* For purposes of our discussion, the effect of dividends can be ignored.)

Let's assume that IBM is trading at $148 in April, two months prior to June expiration. We already know that, if it were the third Friday in June, these IBM calls would be worth $8. In April, however, these calls are worth more than $8. They're more likely to be trading closer to $11.375. Why? There are really two reasons. First, the owner of the calls doesn't have to lay out $140 for another two months, yet he is entitled to all of the stock's appreciation until June. Think about it. If IBM stock were to gain another $10 per share by June expiration, then IBM would be trading at $158. The owner of stock (since April) would have a gain of $10 on his $148 investment. On the other hand, if the IBM June $140 calls could be purchased for only $8 in April, then the owner of an $8 call option would also make $10 in the same two-month period. (That's because, on the expiration date, the owner of the call could purchase stock at $140 and sell it for $158; after subtracting the $8 initial cost, the profit would be $10.) This result wouldn't be fair.

After all, the owner of the stock laid out an additional $140 for the same amount of profit. The owner of the call received the upside in IBM's stock without having to invest an additional $140. To compensate for this, the amount of interest that could have been earned on the $140 for the two months until expiration should be reflected in the price of the call. It is. Assuming a 6-percent interest rate, the interest earned on $140 would be approximately $1.40 per share. So, in addition to what's known as the *intrinsic value* of the call—the amount by which the call is already *in the money* (in our example, the difference between the market price for IBM of $148 and the exercise price of the call of $140, or $8)—an imputed interest rate for the amount of money the call buyer didn't have to lay out for the two months is also included in the call price. That's how we move from a call price of $8—the intrinsic value of the call—to approximately $9.40—the value of the call including the interest on the $140 the buyer of the call didn't have to lay out.

But I said the call should trade at approximately $11.375. What accounts for the nearly $2 difference between the $9.40 we already figured and the actual price of $11.375? Clearly, there has to be another benefit to owning calls—and there is. The buyer of the call can only lose the amount of money invested in the call. While this doesn't sound all that great, when you compare it to owning the common stock of IBM, it is. This is because, at the June expiration date, if IBM stock falls to $140 per share, the owner of the call loses his original investment of $11.375. If IBM stock falls to $130 per share, the owner of the call loses the same $11.375—at $120 per share, or even $80 per share, the call owner only loses $11.375. Sounding better yet?

It's pretty obvious what happens to the poor owner of IBM stock in this scenario. At a price of $140 at the June expiration date, the IBM holder is down $8 from his April purchase price of $148. At a price of $130 in June, he's out $18; if IBM's at

$120 he's out $28; and at a price of $80—the loss gets really ugly—he's out $68 per share. See, there is an added benefit to owning the calls—it's the benefit of not losing any more money after the stock falls below the strike (or exercise) price of $140 per share. What's that worth? Well, in this case, it's probably worth about $2. So, if you pay the $2 in "protection money" as part of the purchase price of the calls, then your cost of $9.40 moves closer to the $11.375 price we talked about before. The $2 cost for assuming the risk below $140 is actually the same as the cost of the put option (but I said we'd only talk about calls—so not another word).

The bottom line is that buying calls is like borrowing money to buy stock, but with protection. The price of the call includes your borrowing costs and and the cost of your "protection"—so you're not getting anything for free, but you *are* leveraging your bet on the future performance of a particular stock. You are also limiting the amount you can lose on the bet to the price of the call.

So, getting back to the main point (the whole "create your own recap" thing), owning a call isn't too much different from owning a stub stock. With a stub stock, you have a leveraged bet on the future of a company, and you can only lose the amount invested in the stub. In our original example, where the company with a $36 stock recapitalized by distributing $30 to its shareholders, the result was a leveraged stub that magnified changes in the value of the underlying company. There, a relatively modest 20-percent increase in earnings resulted, in one scenario, in an 80-percent gain in the stub stock's price.

On the other hand, if the company declared bankruptcy, an owner of the stub stock was only at risk for the amount invested in the stub, not for the $30 of debt taken on by the company to complete the recapitalization.

Despite the similarity between the leverage characteristics of stub stocks and options, the two types of securities differ in one important way. Options have a limited life; they only have value until their expiration date. Stub stocks are common stocks so in some sense, they are really like calls without an expiration date (although the stub stock may become worthless as a result of a bankruptcy proceeding). It is this unlimited life that makes stub stocks so attractive. That's why buying LEAPS, which are merely long-term options, can be an attractive way to emulate a stub stock investment.

While LEAPS don't have an unlimited life like stub stocks, they can usually be purchased up to two and a half years before they expire. This often gives ample opportunity for the stock market to recognize the results from an extraordinary corporate change (like a spinoff or restructuring) or a turnaround in fundamentals (like an earnings gain or the resolution of an isolated or one-time problem). Additionally, two and a half years is often enough time for many just plain cheap stocks either to be discovered or to regain popularity. Since current tax law favors holding investments for more than one year, buying LEAPS is also a way to receive long-term capital gains treatment while receiving the leverage benefits of an option investment.

In some ways, though, LEAPS can't duplicate the dynamics

of a well-planned recap. In a recap, management and employ-ees can be incentivized using the new stub stock. Given the tremendous upside of stub stocks, this can be a powerful way to unleash the forces of management and employee stock owner-ship in an organization. Also, a recapitalized company has the immediate benefit from the tax advantages of a leveraged bal-ance sheet. Obviously, buying LEAPS doesn't affect the tax status of a corporation. (However, because there is an implied interest cost factored into the price of the LEAPS, interest ex-pense does get included in the LEAPS holder's tax basis.)

On the other hand, there is one huge advantage that LEAPS have over stub stocks. You can trade LEAPS on hundreds of companies, while the list of available stub stocks is limited to the number of companies that choose to recapitalize. Even in the 1980s, this list covered only a select few companies at any one time. The fact that there are so many LEAPS to choose from—and that *you*, rather than a company's management, get to choose which stocks would make the best leveraged (or "stub-like") investments—should make LEAPS a very useful investment alternative.

While stub stock opportunities are generally easy to spot, as there is usually an announced recapitalization transaction, in-vestments in LEAPS come about in a different way. In most cases, your decision to invest in LEAPS will simply be a by-product of your ongoing research efforts. Before you even begin thinking about LEAPS, a special situation or an under-valued stock will catch your attention as an attractive invest-ment in its own right. Only after an investment passes this first hurdle will you bother to check whether a chosen investment situation has LEAPS available for trading. At the very least, being able to compare the risk/reward of a stock with the opportunities available through an investment in the related LEAPS will provide you with another good investment choice.

How much money can you make investing in LEAPS? Plenty. But don't take my word for it. Seeing is believing. So let's take a peek at what the potent one-two punch of LEAPS— leverage and extended timing—can do to magnify the returns of good investment ideas in the real world.

CASE STUDY
WELLS FARGO LEAPS

Remember what I told you about stealing other people's ideas? (You know: it's a big world out there; you can't cover everything yourself; you still have to do your own homework.) Well, in the next chapter we'll get around to discussing where to steal from—the short list of publications, newsletters and money managers that I've found to be the most valuable sources of good ideas. However, before we get to that, let's take a look at a situation that I "stole" from one of my favorite investment newsletters, *Outstanding Investor Digest (OID)*. After reading an incredibly compelling investment case for investing in Wells Fargo stock outlined in the newsletter, I concluded this was an idea I had to steal. Only I liked it so much that I decided to leverage my returns through investing in the company's LEAPS. In this case, because of the added element of protection that the LEAPS afforded, I was able to make a great risk/reward situation even better.

In December 1992, I read an interview conducted by *OID* with an investment manager at Lehman Brothers who was previously unknown to me, Bruce Berkowitz. The fact that I had no idea who he was didn't matter. The logic and clarity of the investment case he made for Wells Fargo stock was overwhelming on its own. At that time, Wells Fargo, a large California-based bank, was trading at around $77 per share. California was in the middle of the worst real estate recession since the 1930s. Wells Fargo had by far the largest concentration of commercial real estate loans of any bank in California. According to Berkowitz, BankAmerica, Wells's largest competitor in California, had commercial real estate loans on its balance sheet equal to only $48 per share (its stock price was approximately $47 per share). Wells Fargo, on the other hand, had commercial real estate loans totaling about $249 per share (as compared to a stock price of about $77). Further, Wells had taken a loss provision (reserves that anticipate future loan losses) of $27 per share the previous year, wiping out almost all of its earnings. In just the first nine months of 1992, Wells had provisioned for an additional $18 per share of losses. Many investors questioned whether Wells Fargo would survive the real estate downturn.

Berkowitz's investment case was fairly simple. If you excluded the loss provisions, Wells (adjusting for cash earnings and one-time expenses) was already earning nearly $36 per share before taxes. If the real estate environment ever recovered to a more normalized level, loan-loss provisions, based on past experience, would probably fall to approximately $6 per share on an annualized basis. This would translate to normalized pretax earnings of $30 per share, or $18 per share in earnings on an after–tax basis (assuming a 40-percent tax rate). At a price of nine or ten times earnings, Wells Fargo could be trading at $160 to $180 per share (versus its then current price of $77). The question wasn't how Wells Fargo could increase its earnings power to reach $18 per share in after-tax earnings. Wells was *already* earning that kind of money—but for the effect of the extraordinary loan-loss provisions. According to Berkowitz, the real question was: What was the right way to look at the loan-loss provisions and how bad were they?

Berkowitz explained that the financial position of Wells Fargo was actually quite strong. Even the loans that Wells had already classified on its balance sheet as "nonperforming" were actually earning interest for the bank (although, to be conservative, this interest was not included in the bank's reported earnings). Nonperforming loans are loans that are in some way substandard—either loans that are not paying any interest, not paying the full interest obligation, or loans where it is merely anticipated that future interest charges and principal payments *might* not be met on a timely basis. Far from being worthless, these nonperforming loans, which equaled approximately 6 percent of Wells's total loan portfolio, still had a cash yield of 6.2 percent. This meant that at a time when the prime rate (the interest rate that the bank's best customers paid on their loans) was 6 percent and the cost of Wells's money (the rate Wells paid its depositors) was only around 3 percent, the "questionable" part of Wells's loan portfolio was still earning a very respectable cash return of over 6 percent.

In other words, if Wells was still able to collect such large interest payments from these "nonperforming" loans, maybe they weren't so terrible after all. At least, it made sense that a good portion of the face value of the nonperforming loans' value would ultimately be recovered. In fact, according to Berkowitz, Wells was being so conservative about classifying its loans that 50 percent of those loans it had classified as nonperforming were still up-to-date on all required interest and principal payments.

Further, for purposes of reporting income and taking reserves against its balance sheet, Wells had already assumed the worst for its portfolio of nonperforming loans. Including the hefty loss provisons of the previous two years, reserves for future loan losses stood at 5 percent of the bank's total loan portfolio. Since currently only 6 percent of Wells's loans were classified as "nonperforming" (remember, these loans were far from a total loss), before this 5-percent reserve would become inadequate, either almost all of the nonperforming loans would have to become completely worthless or the loans that were now considered "performing" would have to take a dramatic turn for the worse. Given the level of Wells's apparent conservatism, the way Berkowitz had it figured, both seemed highly unlikely.

Two other points clinched the deal for me. The first was a comparison made in the *OID* piece between Wells Fargo and BankAmerica. According to most investors, BankAmerica's stock was the much more conservative investment of the two banks. As it turned out, however, although Wells did have a much bigger exposure to the California real estate market (and therefore more nonperforming loans), it had already reserved for much bigger losses than BankAmerica. Despite these reserves, Wells Fargo still had higher capital ratios than BankAmerica (tangible equity to total assets, etc.), even after adjusting for its riskier asset profile. This was just another sign that Wells wasn't in as bad shape as the stock market apparently believed.

The second point was even more persuasive. With all of the nonperforming loans, loss reserves, and actual loan losses, Wells Fargo still hadn't shown a loss for any year in its 140-year history. Most industrial companies don't have anywhere near that level of predictability to their earnings. In what many considered to be the worst real estate environment for California in over fifty years, Wells had still managed to eke out a profit in 1991. This indicated to me that Wells was a good bet to get through this difficult period and that a multiple of nine or ten times normalized earnings (an earnings multiple substantially below most industrial companies) was a reasonable and attainable goal for its stock. The bottom line was, if Wells survived the current real estate downturn and its annual loss provisions returned to normalized levels, the stock looked like a potential double.

While the whole analysis made tremendous sense, I did have some nagging concerns. What did I know about the California real estate market? What if the environment in California turned dramatically worse? It appeared as though Wells could weather a pretty severe storm, but what if the once-in-fifty-years rain turned into an unprecedented monsoon? Of course, I never invest in situations with complete certainty, anyway. Situations that make sense and offer attractive returns given the risks involved—that's all I can really ask for.

But still—a bank is a funny animal. You never really know exactly what makes up its loan portfolio. The financial statements only give a very general overview of the bank's assets. Then again, Wells did offer some comfort in this area. Between its reserves, the "quality" of its nonperforming loans, and especially its ability to earn huge returns each year, Wells seemed to have a huge cushion to cover any future loan losses. Nevertheless, there was still a chance, no matter how slight, that the bank's portfolio of real estate loans could spoil what looked like a great investment.

That's why investing in the LEAPS seemed to make such good sense. Although the stock looked like an outstanding investment—combining a great chance for a double with a remote possibility of disaster—the LEAPS looked even better. At that time (December 1992), I could buy Wells Fargo

LEAPS that gave me the right to buy stock at $80 per share until January 1995—more than two years away. By the time those two years were up, I figured it would be pretty clear whether or not Wells had survived the California real estate crisis. If things were looking up by then, there was an excellent chance that Wells's earning power would be reflected in its stock price; a price of $160 or more didn't seem outlandish. On the other hand, if the severe downturn turned into a real estate debacle, the stock could trade substantially below $80. And in the absolute worst case, there would be a government takeover of the bank with the stockholders wiped out.

With that outlook, and at a price of $14, the January 1995 calls (referred to as LEAPS because of their long duration) to buy Wells Fargo stock at $80 per share looked pretty enticing. These LEAPS would give me the right to buy Wells Fargo stock at $80 per share until they expired in January 1995. If Wells were trading at $160 by then, these LEAPS would skyrocket to $80—because I could buy Wells at $80 and immediately sell it for $160. On an investment of $14, this would mean a profit of $66, or a gain representing almost five times my original investment. If Wells crashed and burned, I would be out just the $14. So, one way to look at an investment in the LEAPS was: here was a way to set up a risk/reward ratio of 1 down to almost 5 up.

The stock, if you looked at this extreme scenario (Wells was either going to make it with flying colors or not make it at all), did not offer as good of a risk/reward. At a price of $77 per share, if the stock hit $160, stockholders would make a little more than $80. If Wells didn't make it, a stockholder could lose almost $80. This was a bet of 1 up to 1 down. Since the fact situation outlined in the *OID* interview seemed to check out, I was actually pretty excited about the upside prospects for Wells. Right or wrong, my assessment of the chances for the extreme downside case were below 5 percent. While this analysis made both the stock and the LEAPS look like terrific investment opportunities—the LEAPS, under this scenario, provided the better risk/reward.

A simpler case for the LEAPS went this way: If I liked Wells Fargo so much, why couldn't I just leverage up my bet by borrowing money to buy the stock? Well, that's just what I did by buying the LEAPS—only I got a really great deal. Here's how it went: I could borrow the *entire* purchase price of Wells stock in December 1992. The only money I had to lay out up front was for the interest charges on my borrowing. This would represent interest for the next 25 months, taking me to January 1995. The catch was that the interest charges wouldn't be low, though the rates wouldn't be nearly as high as the rates on my credit card. The interest rate would be closer to the borrowing costs of a large corporation with a B or BB investment rating from a major rating agency like Standard & Poor's—i.e., not considered investment grade, but not terrible either.

But here's the good part. I was only on the hook for those up-front interest charges. If the investment in Wells Fargo stock didn't work out (i.e., if the stock traded down—even all the way down to zero), I didn't have to pay off the principal of the loan I took out to buy the stock. My only loss would be those up-front interest charges. On the other hand, if the stock went up, I would participate dollar for dollar in Wells's upside. My profits would be equal to the increase in Wells Fargo's stock less the interest charges for borrowing the money to buy the stock. Hmmm . . . I had to look at this again: Interest rates equivalent to those paid by many large corporations; no repayment obligation on the loan if things didn't work out. That sounded pretty good. My only question was: Where do I sign up? (*Note:* This was no different from a typical LEAPS analysis. The interest costs were high because they included the cost of the "protection money." Also, for you sticklers, including the effect of dividends does not materially change the basic point.)

So what happened? Pretty much everything that Berkowitz had predicted. California didn't fall into the ocean and Wells Fargo earned almost $15 per share in 1994 and over $20 per share in 1995. By September 1994, the stock had more than doubled to $160 per share. As for the LEAPS . . . what's another word for "home run"?

A Quick Word on Warrants

If you liked LEAPS, in some ways *warrants* are even better. A warrant gives the holder the right to buy stock at a specified price for a set period of time. While similar to call options, warrants differ in two ways. First, warrants are issued by the underlying company. So, five-year warrants to buy IBM stock at $82 per share allow the holder to purchase stock directly from IBM at any time during the next five years at a price of $82. In contrast, listed call options represent contractual arrangements between investors to buy or sell a particular stock; the underlying company is not involved.

The second difference between typical call options and warrants should be of more importance to you. At the time they are issued, warrants usually have a longer time-to-expiration than typical call options. Like LEAPS, warrants can extend for a period of years. Though LEAPS usually extend for no more than two and a half years, the expiration date for newly issued warrants can be five, seven or even ten years away. (Some perpetual warrants—with *no* expiration date—have actually been issued.) As with LEAPS, the investment merits of the underlying stock are the main basis for making a warrant investment. Given the benefits of leverage and "protection" offered by warrants over such an extended period of time, it is usually worth checking to see whether warrants have been issued by companies whose stocks appear attractive.

ANOTHER QUICK WORD: OPTIONS AND SPECIAL-SITUATION INVESTING

Warning: This section is for advanced students only (although compulsive gamblers are also welcome). The option markets can present special-situation investors with an opportunity to make spectacular profits from a little-known market inefficiency. This is true even though for over two decades elaborate computer models have been continually developed and refined to calculate the correct theoretical values for every conceivable type of option (including LEAPS and warrants). Given the amount of professional and academic firepower directed toward the study of options and other *derivative* securities (securities created to emulate or react to the movements of other securities), you might think that common sense and a pencil would be of little use. In reality, when it comes to investing in the options of companies undergoing extraordinary corporate change, special-situation investors have a huge advantage over the high-powered *quants* (read "computer-wielding eggheads," or more accurately "rich computer-wielding eggheads").

This is because, in many cases, option traders (including the quants) view stock prices as simply numbers—not as the prices of shares in actual businesses. In general, professionals and academics calculate an option's "correct" or theoretical price by first measuring the past price volatility of the underlying stock—a measure of how much the price of the stock has fluctuated. This volatility measure is then plugged into a formula that is probably some variant of the *Black-Scholes model* for valuing a call option. (This is the formula used by most academics and professionals to value options.)

The formula takes into account the stock's price, the exercise price of the option, interest rates, and the time remaining until expiration, as well as the stock's volatility. The higher a stock's past volatility, the higher the option price. Often, however, option traders who use these formulas do not take into account extraordinary corporate transactions. The stocks of companies undergoing an imminent spinoff, corporate restructuring, or stock merger may move significantly as a result of these special transactions—not because historically their stocks have fluctuated in a certain way. Therefore, the options of companies undergoing extraordinary change may well be mispriced. It should be no surprise, then, that this is where your opportunity lies.

Depending upon how large or how important a spinoff is relative to the parent company, the stocks of spinoffs and parent companies can move dramatically after a spinoff is completed. Since the date of distribution of spinoff shares is announced in advance, knowing this information along with some fundamental information about the underlying companies involved can give you a large edge over option traders who invest "by the numbers." One strategy would be to buy options that expire several weeks to several months after a spinoff is consummated. In the period after the spinoff, the parent company's stock may make a dramatic move because investors had previously been holding back on purchasing the parent's stock until the divestiture of the unwanted business was completed. So, too, the spinoff stock's price could be a source of surprise during this initial trading period simply because it is a new stock with no trading history and no underwriter to set an expected price range. The bottom line is that the options markets can be a profitable place to exploit your research efforts in the spinoff area. Specifically, you can apply both your knowledge of when a spinoff is scheduled to take place and your fundamental understanding of the underlying companies involved.

Restructuring transactions and stock mergers can provide similar advantages to knowledgeable option investors. In restructuring situations, knowing the timing of crucial events in an ongoing program can help you choose the appropriate option expiration date for a call or put position. In many cases, the date of a significant distribution of cash or securities or the target date for the sale of assets can correspond to a significant price move in the underlying stock.

In merger situations, where a portion of the acquisition price is paid with common stock, it is the closing date of the merger that can be the catalyst for extraordinary stock price moves. Shares of the acquiring company (into which your options on the target company become convertible once the merger is completed) are under all sorts of pressure before and immediately after the merger is finalized. First, in most cases, risk arbitrageurs start buying shares of the target company and simultaneously begin shorting shares of the acquirer almost immediately after a merger is announced. Only once the merger is completed is this source of selling pressure on the acquirer's stock usually relieved. Also, in the weeks immediately after the closing of a merger, those shareholders who had not already sold their shares when the merger was announced tend to sell the shares they received in the acquirer's company. This is usually because the original investment in the target company's shares was made for reasons specific to that company—reasons not applicable to the acquirer's shares. After this selling pressure subsides, the acquirer's stock can sometimes move up dramatically. This is most apt to take place when a large amount of new stock is issued in the merger relative to the amount of predeal shares the acquirer had outstanding.

But enough theory. Now, let's see a real-world example of how extraordinary corporate events can throw a wrench into the workings of the most sophisticated computer models.

CASE STUDY

MARRIOTT CORPORATION OPTIONS

The Marriott spinoff situation (discussed in chapter 3) provides a good example of this phenomenon. As we saw, Marriott Corporation was splitting into two separate companies—a "good" Marriott (Marriott International) and a "bad" Marriott (Host Marriott). Marriott International was expected to have all of the valuable hotel-management contracts and Host Marriott was expected to hold all of the unsalable real estate burdened with billions in debt. With almost eleven months' prior warning, the split was scheduled to take place on September 30, 1993.

In August of 1993, with Marriott Corporation stock trading at $27.75, I was able to purchase the October 1993 calls with an exercise price of $25 per share for a cost of $3.125. Since the third Friday in October fell on October 15th (and the spinoff was to be completed by September 30), the stocks of both Marriott International and Host Marriott would be trading independently for at least two weeks before my calls expired. Usually, if a spinoff takes place before an option expires, upon exercise the option holder is entitled to receive shares in both the parent company and the spinoff as if he had owned stock on the spinoff date. In this particular case, this meant that if I exercised my calls when they expired in the middle of October, I would receive one share of Marriott International and one share of Host Marriott in exchange for the exercise price of $25.

The trick was that the price I paid for my options didn't take into account the fact that a spinoff was being consummated several weeks before their expiration. Both stocks, the parent and the spinoff, would be trading independently before my options expired. Investors who had been waiting to purchase the "good" Marriott (Marriott International) without taking on the risks of all that debt and unsalable real estate would finally be able to buy the stock in the first two weeks of October. This could mean a significant price move during the new stock's first weeks of trading.

Further, the valuation of the "bad" Marriott (Host Marriott) was also in question. Host Marriott had over $2.5 billion of debt and little more than 100 million shares outstanding. Therefore, the difference between a stock price of $3 per share for Host Marriott and a price of $6 per share was not as large as it might have appeared. A $3 share price would mean a total market capitalization (the total market value of debt plus stock) of $2.8 billion, and a $6 stock price would translate into a total market capitalization for the company of $3.1 billion — a valuation differential of only 10 percent rather than the apparent 100-percent disparity. In short, the first two weeks of October were going to be a very active time for the stocks of both Host Marriott and Marriott International.

What happened? Well, approximately a month after my initial purchase of the options, just days before the September 30 spinoff date, the stock of Marriott Corporation had moved up to $28.50, resulting in a price for the October 25 calls of $3.625. However, by October 15th, the date my options expired, a dramatic change had taken place. Host Marriott stock was trading at $6.75. The stock of Marriott International traded up to $26 per share. Since my options gave me the right to buy one share of both stocks for a combined price of $25, my options had skyrocketed to $7.75. This was because the value of one share of Marriott International at $26 plus one share of Host Marriott at $6.75 equaled a combined value of $32.75 (which I had the right to buy at $25). The rise in the October 30 calls was even more dramatic. These calls, which could have been purchased for $.25 on September 23, were worth $2.75 upon expiration just three weeks later.

There is no way that plugging past price volatilities into a computer program could have predicted this dramatic move in the options of Marriott Corporation. See how a little work and a little knowledge can pay off? Isn't it nice to know that, every now and again, life *is* fair?

A Quick Summary and a Free Offer

1. Stub Stocks.   There is almost no other area of the stock market where research and careful analysis can be rewarded as quickly and as generously.

2. LEAPS.   There is almost no other area of the stock market (with the possible exception of stub stocks) where research and careful analysis can be rewarded as quickly and as generously.

3. Warrants and Special Situation Option Investing. There is almost no other area of the stock market (with the possible exception of stub stocks and LEAPS) where research and careful analysis can be rewarded as quickly and as generously.

Free Offer

‒ ·‒ ·‒ ·‒ ·‒ ·‒ ·‒ ·‒ ·‒ ·‒ ·‒ ·‒ ·‒ ·‒ ·‒ ·‒ ·‒

Free   **Free**

This coupon entitles the bearer to one free set of

GINSU KNIVES

(Coupon must be accompanied by 5 [five] trade confirmations of now worthless stub stocks, LEAPS, warrants, or options)

This offer is void and prohibited. Offer expires the third Friday of each month. Please allow 6 to 8 weeks for delivery—then wait some more.

Free ‒ ·‒ ·‒ ·‒ ·‒ ·‒ ·‒ ·‒ ·‒ ·‒ ·‒ ·‒ ·‒ ·‒ **Free**

Chapter 7

SEEING THE TREES
THROUGH THE FOREST

So, am I that crazy cop, the one whose partner's always getting killed? You know, I keep making money investing in all of these special corporate situations while you end up in a fetal position wearing an old pair of feety pajamas? Well, the truth is, I could be that cop. Whether I am or not is largely up to you.

While it's true that you *can* be a stock market genius, there's no guarantee that you *will* be. Like the acquisition of any new skill, becoming a good investor can take both time and practice. By leading you to investment areas where the odds are stacked in your favor, I've tried to give you a big head start. But you still have to use good judgment. If you're not already an experienced stock-market investor, you might start off investing only a small portion of your assets in these special corporate situations. As your experience and knowledge expand, you may feel confident enough to commit a larger share of your resources.

There are other ways you can avoid playing the role of the "dead partner." Frankly, I'm not going to be around to avenge your death in Act III, so you're going to have to learn how to look out for yourself. One way to do this is to pay attention to the make-up of your portfolio. For instance, while a portfolio of five or six different spinoffs probably makes sense, a portfolio made up solely of five or six different LEAPS probably doesn't. Similarly, unless you're an expert in the field, concentrating all or most of your investments in any one industry is generally unwise. Further, taking on lots of margin debt can force you to sell out your positions at just the wrong time; only investors with substantial experience should borrow more than modest amounts against their investment portfolio. But all of this is just common sense. If you're short on common sense when it comes to investments—and you aren't willing to put in the time to get some—maybe managing your own portfolio isn't for you.

When it comes right down to it, this book can't help you with a lot of the decisions you'll have to make in your investment life. I'm no expert on insurance, annuities, commodities, real estate (although selling *me* real estate seems to be a good strategy), rare coins, oil wells, or dog racing. I do know about special-situation investing in the stock market—and I don't know of any place to get better returns—consistently and over a long period of time. That's why the vast majority of my investments are concentrated in this area. However, just because this strategy makes sense for me doesn't make it right for you. How much of your investment funds end up in these special stock situations depends on your individual financial needs, your knowledge of other investment areas—and—how well you learn to apply the information in this book.

While all of the "market-beating" strategies we've discussed can help you make (or increase) your fortune, some areas are easier to get started with than others. For instance, everyone can play the spinoff game. Spinoffs are easy to spot. You can pick and choose from a large number of opportunities. The bargains will keep coming—just because of the way the "system" works. And since the group as a whole beats the pants off the market, you can even bungle your way to some pretty nice profits. The other great thing is that you can spend your whole life just in the spinoff area (of course, eventually no one will talk to you and pretty soon the drool dripping off your chin can start to bug you)—but there's really no need to look anywhere else. Remember, if investing in spinoffs is what works best for you, by all means, keep doing it until they cart you away.

On the other hand, there are a few areas, like LEAPS and special-situation options, where everyone, especially those just getting started with options, should use more than the usual amount of caution. While even investing a small portion of your assets in these highly leveraged instruments can lead to a spectacular increase in the worth of your entire portfolio, options carry a particularly high degree of risk. Investing in this area without a good understanding of how options work is like running through a dynamite factory with a burning match—you may live, but you're still an idiot.

No matter where you choose to get started, keep in mind, an entire portfolio won't materialize overnight. However, even if you only spot an attractive situation every two or three months, you should still be able to build a respectable portfolio of special-investment situations within approximately a year. At that rate, over a two-year period you'll probably have made eight to ten different investments (although a lesser number are likely to be in your portfolio at any one time). Under normal circumstances, you won't end up with a portfolio of just merger securities or orphan stocks or companies going through a restructuring. If you are truly going to pick your spots — sticking to the situations that you understand well and that offer extraordinary risk/reward characteristics — one or two good opportunities from each of these areas will be a more typical experience.

As I mentioned earlier, spinoffs are a different story. In recent years, there have been so many opportunities in the spinoff area that it *would* be possible to create an entire portfolio of just spinoffs (especially if you throw in some parent companies too). So finding three, four, or even five of these situations over a two-year period should pose little problem. While you'll have even more opportunities to invest in LEAPS (since LEAPS are always trading on hundreds of companies), investing more than 10 or 15 percent of your portfolio in these instruments at any one time would, because of their leveraged nature, almost always be ill advised.

Here's another way you can play. You don't have to make

up your entire portfolio out of these special corporate situations. Maybe you have another strategy that works for you. Let's say you're a Ben Graham fan. You don't want to put in the time or effort to pick individual stocks, but you still have a hankering to beat the market. Putting together a group of fifteen or twenty stocks that trade at low prices relative to their book value and also at low price/cash-flow ratios will probably do the job. If you pepper this portfolio with the occasional special-situation investment (accounting for maybe 20 or 30 percent of the total pie), you can still get very satisfying results. While I'm not a huge fan of statistical investing (because I always figure I'll do better by researching and understanding the businesses I'm buying), for do-it-yourself investors with limited time this might be an acceptable strategy.

But, however it happens, let's assume you're hooked. Special-situation stock investing is the thing for you. You're ready to roll up your sleeves and get to work. What do you do now? Where do you look to find these special investment opportunities? What information sources will be helpful once you find them? What if you need to brush up on the basics? Where can you get up to speed on the fundamentals of accounting—things like balance sheets, income statements, and cash flow? Well, first—stop asking so many questions. Then, I'll be happy to make the answers to the ones you've already asked (and more) the subject of the rest of this chapter.

Answer: Read, read, read.

While you might not think that a newspaper with a circulation in the millions would be a good place to hunt for bargains off the beaten path, it turns out that it is. In fact, *The Wall Street Journal* is the hands-down winner for Best Source of new investment ideas. Many big money-making opportunities (including most of the examples in this book) appear at one time or another right on the front page—sometimes for months at a time. Even though transactions and corporate changes that involve smaller companies may not make the front page, they're still in there. It's not that no one else will see this news, but after reading this book, *you* now have a better idea what to look for.

The battle to acquire Paramount Communications made front-page headlines for nearly six months—but the final method of payment did not. Cash, stock, and four obscure securities just don't make headlines. Although *The Wall Street Journal* discloses this information, they don't focus on it. You will. Likewise, while the spinoff of some small division used to be of minor concern, now it will seem like a major event. Even the word "bankruptcy" will have a certain cachet when you spot it in the morning paper. But you get the idea: While others will just be reading the words, you'll be finding new investment opportunities between the lines.

You don't have to read anything other than *The Wall Street Journal*, though you can find new ideas almost anywhere in the business press. Time and interest are your only constraints. Particularly good newspapers for scouting out new ideas include the *New York Times, Barron's,* and *Investor's Business Daily.* Your local paper and regional business paper can also be good hunting grounds for special situations. This is because extraordinary transactions involving local companies and their subsidiaries are often covered locally in greater detail, with more background, and for a longer period of time than the same events in papers of a more national scope. Additionally, industry-specific newspapers like *American Banker* or *Footwear News* can be helpful, but if you don't already get one—don't bother.

There's also the list of well-known business magazines to choose from. I've found *Forbes* and *Smart Money* to be the best sources of good ideas. However, *Business Week, Fortune, Financial World, Worth, Money, Kiplinger's Personal Finance,* and *Individual Investor* can also be worth reading. You certainly can't (and don't want to) read everything so, just as you do with stocks, pick your spots. Remember, it's the quality of your ideas, not the quantity, that will result in the big money. So don't kill yourself; read when you have time and when you're in the mood. That way, you'll end up being much more productive.

If I haven't yet given you enough to read, the next source of potential ideas is investment newsletters. These are letters that come out on a periodic basis whose annual subscription prices usually run somewhere between $50 and $500. While investment newsletters generally deserve their bad reputation, I've narrowed the field down to a short list of publications that can be a particularly fertile ground for new investment ideas. My favorite, which I've already mentioned, is *Outstanding Investor Digest* (phone: 212-777-3330). *OID* interviews mostly top-notch, value-oriented investment managers who discuss their best ideas in a usually cogent and understandable way. This letter is particularly good for finding potential LEAPS candidates and occasionally for learning about companies that are undergoing or have recently completed a re-structuring.

Another good investment letter, *The Turnaround Letter* (phone: 617-573-9550), covers companies that, as the name implies, are undergoing some kind of corporate turn-around. Two of the main focuses of this letter are orphan stocks that have recently emerged from bankruptcy pro-ceedings and stocks in restructuring mode. While this letter is a helpful source of good ideas, it should be used only as a starting point. As always, you still have to do your own work. That goes double for my next suggestion, the *Dick Davis Digest* (phone: 954-467-8500). This is simply a se-lected sampling of what the newsletter's editor feels are the best ideas from a host of other stock-market letters. Scan-ning this letter is a good way to spot an occasional special-investment situation that you may have missed in your other sources.

COPYING THE MASTERS

Here's another way to ferret out some new investment ideas. This one takes a phone call and a small amount of investigative work. You can get a copy of the stock portfolios of some of the best special-situation and value investors in the country by simply calling. The prospectuses for the funds in one of the top mutual-fund groups in the United States, the *Mutual Series Funds* (phone: 800-448-3863), can be an excellent hunting ground for ideas. About 25 percent of this fund group's portfolios concentrate on companies undergoing extraordinary corporate changes. Michael Price, who manages the funds, is a well-known (and outstanding) value and special-situation investor. Of course, you'll still have to look through a rather extensive portfolio to figure out which securities were purchased as a result of a past or pending significant corporate event. Concentrating on those special situations that are still close to Mr. Price's average cost (disclosed in the prospectus) might be a good place to start.

Marty Whitman's *Third Avenue Value Fund* (phone: 800-443-1021) provides similar opportunities for investors to pirate good ideas. Mr. Whitman is a long-time Wall Street pro who specializes in value-oriented investment situations that are unique and off the beaten path. The newest fund on the list, the *Pzena Focused Value Fund* (phone: 800-385-7003), is run by Richard Pzena, the former director of U.S. equities at S. C. Bernstein & Co. As this fund concentrates mostly on out-of-favor large-capitalization value stocks, it can be an excellent source for good LEAPS ideas. Mr. Pzena's three or four largest holdings (position size is also disclosed in the prospectus) would probably be a good place to start. (*Note:* While I do own shares in Mr. Pzena's firm, since I'm telling you to steal his best ideas, I'm hoping any potential conflicts even out.)

The concept of choosing from a preselected list of stocks makes sense—especially when those stocks already sit in a top investor's portfolio. But remember, you only need one good idea every once in a while. It's better to do a lot of work on one idea than to do some work on a lot of ideas. Whether you go prospecting for ideas in *The Wall Street Journal* or in the portfolios of a mutual fund, most of the time, even after you've researched a situation, you'll still come up dry. Maybe a particular investment situation won't offer you the "margin of safety" you need. Maybe it won't have the upside prospects you'd like. But mostly you'll come up dry because you don't understand the specific situation—the company's industry, the competition, or the effects of an extraordinary change. But that's okay. You're only looking for a handful of special situations that you feel confident about. So don't get overwhelmed looking for new ideas. Reading the paper every day is just fine. Now that you have a better idea what you're looking for, the ideas will come anyway.

OK—You've Got an Idea! Now What?

Primary Sources of Investment Information

Once you've found a potentially interesting special situation, there are a number of places you can turn to for further information. The primary source of investment information is provided by the company itself. The Securities and Exchange Commission (SEC) requires that all the publicly traded companies under its supervision make certain periodic and special filings.

For background information, the ones you'll be most interested in are the company's annual report (SEC Form 10K) and the company's quarterly filings (SEC Form 10Q). These reports provide information about the company's business and operating results as well as the most recent income statements, balance sheets, and statements of cash flow. Also, almost anything you might want to know about executive stock ownership, stock options, and overall compensation can usually be found in the company's annual proxy statements (Schedule 14A).

For extraordinary corporate events, these are the filings to look out for:

Form 8K This form is filed after a material event occurs such as an acquisition, asset sale, bankruptcy, or change in control.

Form S1, S2, S3, and S4 Forms S1 through S3 are the registration statements for companies issuing new securities.

249

Form S4 is filed for securities being distributed through a merger or other business combination, exchange offer, recapitalization, or restructuring. This filing can sometimes be combined with a proxy statement in situations where a shareholder vote is required. (S4's are usually extensive and very informative.)

Form 10 This is the form used to supply information on a spinoff distribution (everything you ever wanted to know about a spinoff but were afraid to ask).

Form 13D This is the report where owners of 5 percent or more of a company must disclose both their holdings and their intentions regarding their stake. If the stake is held for investment purposes, it may be helpful to examine the reputation of the investor making the filing. If the investment was made for the purpose of exerting control or influence over the subject company, this filing may be the first sign of, or serve as a catalyst to, an extraordinary corporate change.

Form 13G Institutional shareholders can file this form, in lieu of a 13D, if the investment is for investment purposes only.

Schedule 14D-1 This is a tender offer statement (see Glossary) filed by an outside party. This document provides much useful background information on a proposed acquisition. You can usually get these from the *information agent* listed in the advertisement announcing the tender offer.

Schedule 13E-3 and 13E-4 The 13E-3 is the filing used for a *going private* transaction (such as the Super Rite transaction in chapter 4). The 13E-4 is the tender offer statement when a company is buying back its own shares (used in the General Dynamics self tender in chapter 5). Remember, both of these situations can be quite lucrative and the disclosures are even more extensive than usual, so read carefully.

In many instances, you can obtain these filings for free (or for a small charge) by calling the company's investor-relations department directly (all right, you might have to fib a little and say you're a shareholder). However, all of these filings are now available free of charge over the Internet through the EDGAR system. Every company is now required to file its disclosure documents electronically through the EDGAR system. (EDGAR is an acronym for Electronic Data Gathering Analysis and Retrieval.) These filings are available through two free Web sites within twenty-four hours of their original filing with the SEC. This should be perfectly fine for almost all of your needs. Currently, New York University provides a free Web site at http://edgar.stern.nyu.edu/edgar. html and the SEC also has a site at http://www.sec.gov/edgarhp.html.

New services and information sources are being added to the on-line world each day. One of the more affordable services for individual investors is EDGAR Online (http://www.edgar-online.com/). If you simply must have those filings right away, this site can get you documents within minutes of their filing with the SEC. A basic service starts at as little as $9.95 per month. Also, Prodigy, Compuserve, and America Online have varying levels of pay-as-you-go original-document services.

There are also document services such as Disclosure (phone: 800-874-4337), Moody's (phone: 800-342-5647), Standard & Poor's (phone: 212-208-8000), Federal Filings (phone: 888-333-3453), Docutronics Information Services (phone: 212-233-7140), and the CCH Washington Service Bureau (phone: 800-955-5219) that will print and deliver these documents to your door or fax machine—for a charge. Documents obtained through these high-end services can run from $15 to $35.

SECONDARY SOURCES OF INVESTMENT INFORMATION

Secondary sources of information can also be quite useful to get a quick overview of a particular company or industry. I often use the well-known *Value Line Investment Survey* for this purpose. I don't use the service's investment rankings, but *Value Line*'s individual company reports give a very helpful overview of a firm's historical operating and investment performance. In addition, since *Value Line*'s reports are arranged by industry, it's very easy to obtain industry valuation data for use in valuing spinoff and restructuring candidates. With its new expanded edition, *Value Line* now provides helpful information on over 3,500 companies. The service might be somewhat pricey for individual investors, but most public libraries have at least one copy in their reference section.

Luckily, with the growth of on-line and other computerized services, good investment information is more available and a lot cheaper than it used to be. If you can't get to a *Value Line*, you might check out the Hoover Business Resources area on America Online. Here you can find, classified by name or by industry, the financial and background information on thousands of companies. This type of information is available, in one form or another, on all the major on-line services.

Of course, keeping up with and reviewing recent company news will also be part of your research effort. *The Wall Street Journal* is great, but depending upon when you spot a potential opportunity, sometimes you may need to review some past news stories. Once again, the basic on-line services can do the job, but a more specialized news service, Dow Jones News/Retrieval—Private Investor Edition (phone: 800-522-3567), can come in pretty handy when doing background searches. Don't worry, you don't need a service this powerful to find and research one good idea every few months, but if you're really hooked on these special situations, at $29.95 per month for unlimited evening searches of the Dow Jones newswires, *The Wall Street Journal*, *Barron's*, and hundreds of other publications—it's tough to beat.

Another helpful service gets delivered to your fax every morning. This one's good for both keeping you current on your positions and alerting you to new opportunities. A service called *HeadsUp* from Individual, Inc. (phone: 800-414-1000) can send you a brief summary of news stories affecting your areas of interest. For instance, you can get the day's top stories on topics like "Corporate Restructuring," "Mergers and Acquisitions," and "Corporate Bankruptcy News." This service runs about $30 a month and is also available over the Internet.

But, once again, you don't *need* any of these bells and whistles. *The Wall Street Journal,* a phone to call for company information and news releases, and a library card can do the trick. In most of these cases, you'll have plenty of time to do your work. If a situation is moving so fast that a couple of hours or days make a difference, it's probably not for you. Most of the Wall Street guys you see on television running around yelling and screaming aren't really thinking and doing research. They're—well, I'm not sure what they're doing, but don't *you* worry about it. The important thing is to stick to the few situations that you have time to research and understand.

QUESTION: WHAT IF YOU NEED SOME BRUSHING UP ON THE BASICS? WHERE CAN YOU GET UP TO SPEED UNDERSTANDING THE BASIC FINANCIAL STATEMENTS?

As my father always says, "figures don't lie, but liars can figure." So when it comes to reading balance sheets and income statements, if you want to look out for yourself and you're a little weak on the basics, it's probably a good idea to do a little brush-up work. Nothing major is required. You can get a good enough understanding of balance sheets and income statements from any of the following good (but short) primers: *How to Read a Financial Report* by John A. Tracy; *How to Use Financial Statements* by James Bandler; and *How to Read Financial Statements* by Donald Weiss (this pamphlet-size book is published by the American Management Association and costs about $4).

Unfortunately, my favorite book in this area is no longer in print. The book, *Interpretation of Financial Statements* by Benjamin Graham, is an extremely thin volume of just what you need to know. While it doesn't really matter how you learn the basics, if you can get your hands on a copy from a library or used-book service, it might be worth the effort.

WHAT'S ALL THIS ABOUT CASH FLOW? WHAT IS IT? WHY SHOULD YOU CARE? (HOW CAN YOU GET SOME?)

Cash flow is a term investors define in many different ways. The cash flow measure that I find to be most helpful when analyzing companies is what some people refer to as *free cash flow*. In most cases, free cash flow gives you a better idea than net income of how much actual cash is flowing through a company's doors each year. Since cash earnings (as opposed to reported earnings) can be used to pay dividends, buy back stock, pay down debt, finance new opportunities, and make acquisitions, it's important to be aware of a company's cash-generating ability. The concept is easy enough, and you can get all of the information you need from the *Statement of Cash Flows* found in all of a company's required annual and quarterly financial filings.

The whole idea is that the net income number (usually reported as earnings per share) only reflects a company's income for accounting purposes. Included in net income are certain noncash expenses; on the other hand, certain cash expenses are excluded from the net income calculation. The free cash flow measure simply adds back to net income some of these noncash expenses and deducts some of the cash expenses, to give a more accurate look at how much cash a company is generating.

Primarily, the noncash expenses are *depreciation* and *amortization*. Depreciation is a noncash accounting charge taken against earnings to allocate the cost of fixed assets like plant and equipment over their useful lives. For example, it's not fair to take an expense against earnings of $1 million in the year you spend $1 million on a new machine, if that machine is expected to last for ten years. A charge against earnings of, say, $100,000 per year would be more reflective of the economic reality of the transaction. So even though $1 million in cash went out the door in the first year, the income statement only gets hit with a charge of $100,000, representing one year's worth of depreciation.

Amortization is also a noncash expense similar to depreciation, except that the annual charges to earnings represent the write-down of certain *intangible* assets over a period of time. Intangible assets have a life of one year or more and lack physical substance. *Goodwill* is the most common form of intangible asset. It usually arises as a result of the purchase of a business for a price greater than that company's identifiable assets. This excess cost is placed on the acquirer's balance sheet as goodwill and amortized against income over a period of not more than forty years. In many cases, as long as the earning power of the acquired business doesn't decrease over time, the amortization charge that is deducted from a company's earnings is merely an accounting fiction. (That's why I'm about to add it back to net income.)

To calculate free cash flow in its basic form, you would (1) start with net income, (2) add back the noncash charges of *depreciation and amortization,* (3) then subtract a company's *capital expenditures,* which usually represent cash outlays for investments in new plant and equipment. The result is a measure of how much free cash flow a company generated that year. The calculation looks like this:

Net Income	$20
+ Depreciation	$ 6
+ Amortization	$ 3
	$29
− Capital Expenditures	($ 5)
Free Cash Flow	$24

Notice how, in this example, the free cash flow number is 20 percent greater than the net income number. If, over a period of years, free cash flow were consistently higher than net income, it might be reasonable to rely on the free cash flow number, rather than the net income number, when figuring out the company's value. (I.e., the company would be viewed in terms of a multiple to free cash flow, rather than in terms of the more commonly used multiple to earnings or P/E). Conversely, if a company's free cash flow were consistently lower than net income (and this was not due to a big expansion which required large amounts of capital spending), it might be better to use the more conservative free cash flow number for valuation purposes.

There are several reasons why a company's free cash flow may differ from its reported earnings. One reason is that depreciation (an annual charge based on the *historical* cost of fixed assets) might not accurately reflect the ongoing annual cost of replacing a company's plant and equipment. The cost of replacing this physical plant and equipment may have gone up each year due to inflation. Also, in some businesses, even if the current plant hasn't worn out, it may still be necessary to improve facilities constantly just to keep up with the competition. (For example, a local department store or hotel may need to be renovated sooner than anticipated because of the actions of a crosstown rival or new competitor.) There are also some cases where the depreciation charge is too high to accurately represent ongoing costs. Sometimes technological advances lower the costs of replacement equipment. In other instances, old equipment may last much longer than had been anticipated by the depreciation schedule.

In all of these cases, examining the differences over time between annual depreciation (an accounting estimate of costs) and capital spending (the actual cash cost) can lead you to favor the free cash flow measure over earnings. Once you add back the noncash charges for amortization, the argument for using free cash flow gets even stronger. Since in most healthy businesses amortization is an accounting fiction, it is important to add back the annual amortization charges to get a true picture of a company's cash-generating ability. In cases where annual amortization charges are large, free cash flow is usually a far superior measure of a company's earnings power. (You may recall that this was true in the case of Home Shopping Network's group of television stations, which were later spun off into Silver King Communications.)

One more point. If a company is growing quickly, a high level of capital spending (and therefore a depressed free-cash-flow number) is not necessarily bad news. That portion of capital spending used to maintain already existing facilities is the important issue. Although a few companies disclose the breakdown between maintenance capital spending and capital spending for expansion, usually you must call the company to get this information. In any event, by itself a high capital spending number relative to depreciation is not a cause for concern—if it can be traced purely to the growth of a business that you believe will continue to be successful.

ARE THERE ANY OTHER INVESTMENT BOOKS WORTH READING?

No. (Just kidding.) There are no books that I would recommend that exclusively discuss the special-investment situations found in this book. However, there are books that can give you excellent background information on the stock market and on value investing. All of this information can be helpful when applied to investments in the special-situation area. So, if you have the time and the inclination, here is a list of my all-time favorites:

David Dremen, *The New Contrarian Investment Strategy* (New York: Random House, 1983).

Benjamin Graham, *The Intelligent Investor: A Book of Practical Counsel* (New York: HarperCollins, 1986).

Robert Hagstrom, *The Warren Buffett Way: Investment Strategies of the World's Greatest Investor* (New York: Wiley, 1994).

Seth A. Klarman, *Margin of Safety* (New York: Harper Business, 1991).

Peter Lynch and John Rothchild, *One Up on Wall Street* (New York: Simon & Schuster, 1993) and *Beating the Street* (New York: Simon & Schuster, 1994).

Andrew Tobias, *The Only Investment Guide You'll Ever Need* (revised and updated edition) (New York: Harcourt Brace, 1996).

John Train, *The Money Masters* (New York: HarperCollins, 1994).

Chapter 8

ALL THE FUN'S IN
GETTING THERE

One of my favorite hobbies is sailing—no racing, no destination, just being on the water and sailing. There are faster ways to move on the water—the technology has been out of date for centuries. Certainly there are easier ways to get from one place to another; the ratio of hard work to distance traveled is great. The point, though, is *not* to go anywhere in particular. I always end up just where I started. The point for me is to enjoy and make the most of the journey. All the fun, as the saying goes, has to be in getting there—because there is no "there" there.

To be a successful investor over the long term, you must also pretty much enjoy the journey. Warren Buffett and Peter Lynch long ago surpassed any reasonable level of savings required to ensure that those near and dear to them would be provided for. They clearly enjoy the challenge of investing. If you're the type that's going to lose sleep after the first market dip (or worse yet, if you're going to panic out of your well-thought-out investment positions just because the market falls), then maybe a more passive approach than the one advocated in these pages would be better suited for you. In fact, if you're not going to enjoy the "game," don't bother: there are far more productive uses for your time.

Of course, if you are able to successfully manage your own investments, there can be some side benefits. While everyone knows what money *can't* buy, there are obviously things that money *can* buy: a sense of security, a comfortable retirement, and an ability to provide for your family. Even from a religious standpoint, money doesn't have to be such a bad thing. In fact, if it's used to help others, money can be a very positive force.

Some people—include the renowned eighteenth-century economist Adam Smith in this group—believe that when you pursue your own self-interest, the whole of society benefits. In the stock market, the buying and selling of stocks creates a market for corporate equity and ultimately provides a vehicle for productive businesses to raise capital and expand. While true, this kind of thinking can only go so far. Betting keeps the cashiers employed at the racetrack, but somehow I doubt that Albert Schweitzer pursued this particular style of altruism; there may be a higher and better use for most of your time.

While to many "time is money," it's probably more universal to say that "money is time." After all, time is the currency of everyone's life. When it's spent, the game is over. One of the great benefits of having money is the ability to pursue those great accomplishments that require the gifts of being and time. In fact, you can't raise a family or make your contribution to society without these gifts. So, while money can't buy you happiness or even satisfaction, it might buy you something else. If viewed in the proper light, it can buy you time — the freedom to pursue the things that you enjoy and that give meaning to your life.

This book was meant to be viewed on many different levels. (You'll see what I mean if you take it on an elevator.) If you're an investor who already has substantial stock-market experience, hopefully it has opened up whole new areas of the investment world to you. In many ways, your work should be easier now that you know where to find those special places where the investment odds are so dramatically tilted in your favor. After reading this book, you should also have a better idea what to look for once you get there. For the novice, I hope that this book has served as a first step and as an inspiration. If the opportunities described in this book look enticing, rest assured that most of the areas covered are not beyond the grasp of the average investor. You *don't* have to be a genius, but you *do* need a basic understanding of financial statements, some common sense, and the patience necessary to gain experience.

As I've said all along, it will take some work and some effort, but this knowledge should be comforting to you. If everyone could take advantage of the investment methods described in this book just by showing up, then you probably couldn't expect to achieve extraordinary results. What will set you apart from the crowd will be the same thing that will cause most investors to fall by the wayside. The barrier

267

to stock market success isn't exceptional brain power, unparalleled business savvy (hey, I still own sea-monkeys), or uncommon insight. The secret, now that you know where to look, is in simply doing a little extra work. When you think about it, this seems quite fair.

While it can't be said that life is always fair, in most cases and over the long term the stock market is. Despite being a card-carrying contrarian, I agree with the now widely accepted wisdom that for most people stocks are the investment vehicle of choice. As long as the economy and the individual businesses that make it up continue to grow, sooner or later the stock market will reflect this reality. That doesn't mean that in every period the stock market will provide superior investment returns. Most recently, in a stretch lasting from the late 1960s to the early 1980s, the major market averages hardly advanced at all. But in general and over the long run the stock market will accurately reflect the progress of the businesses that it represents.

Which brings us to the final benefit of the type of special-situation investing that has been the subject of this book. While it's nice and often helpful to have a rising market, it's not required. Because your bargain opportunities are created by special corporate events—events that take place in all market environments—new bargains are constantly being created. In most cases, though, these bargains are only temporary. It might not be today or tomorrow, but if you do your homework well, the stock market will eventually recognize the inherent value that attracted you to the bargain opportunity in the first place. That's why, in the end, a disciplined approach to seeking out bargain stocks will pay off.

The idea behind this book was to let you know about a snowball sitting on top of a hill, to provide you with a map and enough rope and climbing gear so that you can reach that snowball. Your job—should you choose to accept it—is to nudge it down the hill and make it grow.

Appendix

GOTHAM CAPITAL

	Investment Returns since inception	Cumulative Basis $1.00 becomes
1985 (9 mos.)	+ 70.4%	$ 1.70
1986	+ 53.6%	$ 2.62
1987	+ 29.4%	$ 3.39
1988	+ 64.4%	$ 5.57
1989	+ 31.9%	$ 7.34
1990	+ 31.6%	$ 9.66
1991	+ 28.5%	$12.41
1992	+ 30.6%	$16.21
1993	+115.2%	$34.88
1994	+ 48.9%	$51.97

January 1995 *(return of all capital to outside limited partners)*

Annualized return
since inception   + 50.0%

(All returns audited and include portfolio return after all expenses, before general partners' incentive allocation.)

GLOSSARY

AMORTIZATION

A noncash charge to income intended to allocate the cost of intangible assets (assets lacking physical form), such as goodwill or patent rights, over the period of their usefulness. Although the amortization of goodwill (the amount an acquisition price exceeds the fair market value of the identifiable assets being acquired) is charged against income, this expense does not represent an ongoing cash cost. If the value of the acquired business remains stable or increases over time, adding back amortization charges to income will give a clearer picture of a company's true earning power (see the *cash flow* discussion in chapter 7).

BETA

A stock's volatility relative to the overall market. Beta fagetaboutit.

BLACK-SCHOLES OPTION MODEL

A pricing formula developed to place a fair value on options. This model, while useful under normal circumstances, virtually explodes when used to predict the option prices for companies undergoing extraordinary changes (see chapter 6 for details).

BOND

A debt obligation that requires the payment of a specified sum at maturity and that usually requires periodic interest payments. A bond may be senior or junior to other bonds issued by a corporation. It may be subordinated to other debt obligations of a company (having lower priority over a company's assets). It may be a *secured bond* (backed by collateral) or an *unsecured bond* (not backed by collateral), usually referred to as a *debenture*. A bond can be convertible into other securities or be a *zero-coupon bond*, requiring only the payment of principal upon maturity. A *payment-in-kind* or *PIK bond* allows the issuer to make interest payments in the form of additional bonds in lieu of cash.

BOOK VALUE PER SHARE

The value of a company's equity as carried on its balance sheet divided by the number of shares outstanding. *Book value* reflects the historical value of a company's assets less all of the company's liabilities. *Tangible* or *hard book value* excludes the carrying value of a company's intangible assets, such as patents and goodwill. A strategy of buying stocks at low prices relative to their book values has been shown to consistently beat the market.

CAPITALIZATION

see *Market capitalization*

CAPITAL SPENDING

The purchase (or improvement) of fixed assets, such as plant and equipment. *Capital expenditures* are generally depreciated over their useful life, while repairs are expensed in the year made.

CAPITAL STRUCTURE

The make-up of a company's debt and equity. A *debt-to-equity ratio* is one measure used to determine whether a company has a secure or risky capital structure.

CASH FLOW

Defined in various ways. Usually the term *cash flow* is used to refer to a company's cash earnings, consisting of net income plus noncash charges (usually depreciation and amortization). *Free cash flow*, a more useful term because it takes into account a company's capital spending requirements, refers to *net income* plus *depreciation* and *amortization* less *capital spending* (see cash flow discussion in chapter 7).

CONTRARIAN

An investor who is willing to think and act differently from the crowd. (No, it isn't.)

DEBENTURE

see *Bond*.

DEFAULT

Failure to make interest or principal payments on a debt obligation as they come due. Also, *default* refers to the violation of certain loan covenants, e.g., failure to achieve minimum targets of earnings or assets mandated by the lending agreement or bond indenture. This is also where people from Brooklyn believe earthquakes come from.

DEPRECIATION

A noncash charge to income intended to allocate the cost of a fixed asset, such as plant and equipment, over its useful life (see cash flow discussion in chapter 7).

EFFICIENT MARKET THEORY (OR RANDOM WALK THEORY)

A theory suggesting that stocks are efficiently priced and that all publicly available information and future expectations for a stock are reflected in its current price. In its strongest form, this theory proposes that a monkey throwing darts is as likely to outperform the market as a professional investor. (*Note:* Although in general the monkey thing is true, that doesn't mean markets are efficient. This theory is what they teach in business school so that you'll have less competition when doing your own stock research.)

FACE VALUE

The stated value of a bond, note or mortgage as it appears on the face of the instrument or certificate. A debt instrument is usually redeemed for its face value at maturity (the time the debt falls due). A debt instrument may trade (or be issued) above or below its face value.

INDEXING (INDEX FUND)

An investment strategy that seeks to emulate the returns of a particular market index by purchasing most or all of the securities in that index. An S&P 500 index fund would own the 500 stocks that make up the Standard & Poor's 500 index in the proportion used to calculate the index. (This strategy is also known as "giving up.")

FEETY PAJAMAS

Pajamas with attached foot coverings, usually worn by small children or by people who have suffered inordinate stock-market losses.

FIDUCIARY

The person or organization responsible for the proper investing of money entrusted to it for the benefit of a beneficiary (a.k.a. the one who gets sued when something goes wrong with an investment).

FISCAL YEAR

A continuous twelve-month period used by a business as its accounting period. A company's fiscal year may correspond with a calendar year (ending December 31), but many businesses have different fiscal-year ends.

GILLIGAN'S ISLAND

A situation comedy from the 1960s with Gilligan, a millionaire and his wife, a movie star (and the Skipper, too).

INSIDERS

The directors, officers, and key employees of a company; this isn't the complete legal definition of *insiders*, but these are the guys to keep an eye on when making your investment decisions.

INSTITUTIONAL INVESTORS

Organizations that trade large volumes of other people's money; these include pension funds, banks, mutual funds, insurance companies, college endowment funds, and union funds.

LEVERAGE

Financial leverage refers to the amount of debt a company has relative to its equity. A leveraged company will have a high debt/equity ratio. The use of financial leverage can lead to high shareholder returns if a company can earn substantially more on the borrowed money than the cost of the borrowings. A *leveraged investment* is one where the investor borrows money to purchase an investment (e.g., the purchase of a house with a large mortgage or the purchase of stock on margin), or where the investor buys the right to purchase at a later date a relatively large asset for a relatively small amount of money, as in the purchase of an option or warrant.

LEVERAGED BUYOUT

The acquisition of a company using primarily borrowed funds; the acquired company's assets and earnings power are used as the primary basis for the borrowings. You can effectively buy stock in a publicly-traded *leveraged buyout* by investing in stub stocks, leveraged spinoffs, and an occasional merger security.

LIQUIDITY

The ability to buy and sell large volumes of a stock or other security without unduly influencing the security's price. For example, a buyer of 100,000 shares of IBM may be able to purchase those shares in line with the stock's current market price, while a buyer of 100,000 shares of XYZ Donut may force that stock's price substantially higher before finding willing sellers of that amount of stock.

MARGIN DEBT

Borrowing using the value of securities as collateral. Under Regulation T, an individual can borrow up to 50 percent of the market value of qualified stock holdings. People who speculate in the stock market using large amounts of margin debt should refer to the definition of *feety pajamas*.

MARGIN OF SAFETY

The cushion between the price of an asset and its estimated value. Buying securities at a steep discount to their "indicated or appraised" value was the central investment concept outlined by Benjamin Graham.

MARKET CAPITALIZATION (MARKET VALUE)

The value of a corporation determined by multiplying its stock price by the number of its shares outstanding (e.g., a stock with a $17 stock price and 10,000,000 shares outstanding would have a market capitalization of $170 million). Total capitalization would equal the sum of a company's market capitalization plus the value of its outstanding debt.

NASDAQ (NATIONAL ASSOCIATION OF SECURITIES DEALERS AUTOMATED QUOTATIONS SYSTEM)

A computerized system used by brokers and dealers to provide quotations on most over-the-counter (OTC) stocks. Public companies must meet certain minimum requirements to be included in this system.

NONMARKET RISK (UNSYSTEMATIC RISK)

The portion of a stock's risk that is not related to the movement of the market. If you own five to eight stocks in your portfolio (in varied industries) you don't have to worry too much about this.

OPTIONS (LISTED OPTIONS)

The right to buy or sell a security at a specific price for a specified period of time. *Listed stock options* trade in the form of *contracts*. One *contract* represents the right to buy or sell 100 shares of stock. A call option allows the holder to "call away" (or buy) 100 shares of stock at a fixed price on or before a specified date. A *put option* allows the holder to "put" (or sell) 100 shares of stock at a fixed price on or before a specified date. (See chapter 6 for a more comprehensive description of options.) An *incentive stock option* differs from a *listed option*; the former term refers to an option granted by a company to its executives as a form of incentive payment.

Preferred stock

A class of capital stock of a corporation that pays dividends at a specified rate and has preferred status over common stock in the payment of dividends and upon liquidation. A company's preferred-stock obligations are junior to a company's debt obligations. *Preferred stock* may be cumulative; that is, any dividend payments that are missed accumulate and must be fully paid to holders of preferred shares before the common stock may receive dividends. *Preferred stock* may be convertible into other securities, redeemable at a specified price after a specified period of time, or exchangeable at the option of the issuing company for other securities.

Price/earnings ratio (P/E)

The price of a stock divided by its earnings per share; this measure (sometimes referred to as a multiple of earnings) tells you at what multiple a stock is priced relative to its earnings. A stock trading at $10 per share that earns $1 is trading at a P/E of 10. (The reverse of the P/E ratio—or the E/P ratio—is known as the earnings yield. Thus the same stock that has earnings of $1 and a price of $10 would have an earnings yield of 10 percent. It is sometimes easier to use the earnings yield to compare the return of a stock to that of bonds or money-market instruments.)

PRO FORMA FINANCIAL STATEMENT

A hypothetical example of what a balance sheet, income statement, or other financial statement would have looked like if a particular event had already taken place. For example, a *pro forma income statement* might show what a company's earnings would have looked like if a merger had been completed at an earlier date.

PROXY STATEMENT

A document containing certain information required by the Securities and Exchange Commission to be provided to shareholders before they vote on major company matters. For example, a *proxy statement* is distributed to shareholders before directors are elected and before a merger is completed.

RANDOM WALK THEORY

see *Efficient Market Theory*

RISK ARBITRAGE

The purchase of stock in a company that is subject to an announced takeover, sometimes accompanied by the sale of stock in the proposed acquirer. (Why are you reading this? I told you not to try this at home!)

SECURITIES AND EXCHANGE COMMISSION (SEC) FILINGS

The disclosure forms and schedules that public companies are required to file with this government agency; these include periodic reports of financial results as well as disclosures of material company developments.

SHORT SALE

The sale of a borrowed security with the hope that that security will decline before it has to be repurchased—and returned to its owner. This can also refer to an opportunity to make a bargain purchase of pants for warm weather use.

STOCKBROKER

A mix of a lawyer, a politician, and an insurance salesman (but I don't discriminate; some of my best friends are stockbrokers).

STOCK SPLIT

A pro rata increase in the number of outstanding shares of a corporation's stock without any change in the equity or market value of the company. A 3-for-1 split of a $30 stock with 3,000,000 shares outstanding should result in a company with 9,000,000 shares outstanding and a $10 stock. The split, by itself, does not affect the market value of the company.

TENDER OFFER

A publicly advertised offer to purchase some or all of the shares of a company at a stated price; a *tender offer* is usually open for a limited time, and the offer to purchase shares is usually made at a premium to the company's market price. In hostile takeover situations, *tender offers* are often used but rarely viewed tenderly.

UNDERWRITER

An investment banking firm that sells a new issue of securities to the public; the *underwriter* can work alone or with an *underwriting group* or *syndicate*. In a *firm-commitment underwriting,* the investment banker purchases the new securities from the issuing company at a discount and resells the securities at the public offering price.

VILLAGE IDIOT

Someone who spends $24 on an investment book and thinks he can beat the market. (Just kidding.)

VOLATILITY

The size and frequency of price fluctuations; although *volatility* is used as a measure of a stock's risk by most academics, it is generally a poor measure of long-term profitability.

WARRANTS

A security that entitles the holder to buy stock in a company for a specified price and period of time; a *five-year warrant* to buy IBM at $100 per share would allow the *warrant holder* to buy stock directly from IBM for $100 at any time during the next five years.

YIELD TO MATURITY

The rate of return of a bond or other debt instrument if held until its maturity date—the date when the debt becomes due; the *yield to maturity* will differ from the stated interest rate on a debt instrument if it is purchased at a discount or premium to its face value. For example, a 10-percent bond maturing in ten years that is purchased at 80 [at 80 percent of its face value] has a yield to maturity of 13.74 percent. The difference between the *stated yield* and the *yield to maturity* is due to the effect of the annual $10 interest payment on a purchase price of only $80 and the collection of $100 at maturity versus an $80 initial cost.

INDEX

ABOUT THE AUTHOR

Joel Greenblatt is the founder of Gotham Capital, a private investment partnership. In 1994, he became chairman of the board of a *Fortune* 500 company with over $1 billion in annual sales. Greenblatt holds a B.S. and an M.B.A. from the Wharton School. He lives on Long Island and works in Manhattan.